The LEAN
Rotisserie

The LEAN
Rotisserie

No portion of this book may be
reproduced by any means without
permission in writing by the publisher.

Printed in the United States of America

For inquiries contact:
Showtime Kitchens
P.O. Box 4120
Carlsbad, CA 92018
1-888-838-0996

TABLE OF CONTENTS

The LEAN
Rotisserie

4

TABLE OF CONTENTS

The LEAN
Rotisserie

BEEF

LAMB

SEAFOOD

FRUITS & VEGETABLES

The LEAN
Rotisserie

The Lean Rotisserie Cookbook is a collection of recipes with lower fat and calorie content for anyone who is watching their weight or is generally health conscious and using a Ronco Showtime Rotisserie & BBQ.

You can enjoy a wide variety of foods by "Cutting the Fat" at home and making lean and tasty meals your family will love! Healthy rotisserie cooking is easy with a Showtime. Anyone can do it – whether you consider yourself a "cook" or not.

Before electricity, meats were cooked over an open fire on a horizontal spit that turned. Now you can experience the simplicity of spit cooking in your own kitchen. Compared with conventional ovens, the horizontal rotisserie keeps the juices in motion so meats won't dry out. Vertical rotisseries allow the juices and fat to gather at the bottom of the food due to gravity. The top parts become dry and bland. That's why continuous rotating of a horizontal spit is so important to great tasting foods.

A spit is just right when it continuously allows the food to be exposed to the heat source – at a rate that also keeps the food from burning. It also makes the best tasting food taste even better, because you get a lot less fat with even more flavor!

9

The LEAN
Rotisserie

To assist you in choosing recipes that suit your particular dietary needs, **nutrtional information is included** at the bottom of each recipe. This information includes calories, carbohydrates, protein, fat, cholesterol and sodium.

COOKING TIMES AND TEMPERATURES

Please note that the times and temperatures at right are only a guide for your reference and are based on temperatures of refrigerated foods. Rotisseries vary and times will vary due to differences in meat shape, size, and amount of fat and bone. To accurately determine whether food is done, insert a meat thermometer into the thickest sections.

If your poultry is very cold, wash the cavity with warm water to bring the temperature up before placing it on the spit. Caution: If a chicken is partially frozen on the inside, the inner parts may not be completely cooked. Uncooked poultry could carry unwanted bacteria that can make some people ill. Use a meat and poultry thermometer to make sure food is cooked to the minimum safe temperature.

FOOD	WEIGHT/QTY.	INTERNAL TEMP.	TIME
CHICKEN			
Whole Chicken	3-1/2 lbs.	180°	15 min./lb.
Cornish Hens(head over heel)	2-4 hens	180°	10 min./lb.
2 Chickens/Ducks		180°	10 min./lb.
Turkey(unstuffed)	12-15 lbs.	180°	12-15 min./lb.
Chicken Pieces			
with bones	3 lbs.	180°	30-35 min. total
without bones	1-1/2 lbs.	180°	30-35 min. total
Turkey Burgers	1-1/4 lbs.	180° well	30-35 min. total
Chicken Kebobs	6 skewers	180° well	30-35 min. total
PORK			
Rolled Pork Loin	3-1/2 lbs.	160°	20-30 min./lb.
Pork Tenderloin	1-3/4 to 2 lbs.	160°	30-35 min./lb.
Pork Chops	4 chops	160°	30-35 min./lb.
Boneless Pork Chops	6 chops	160°	20 min./lb.
Boneless Ham	3 lbs.	160°	45 nin./lb.
Italian Sausages			
unrotated	up to 20		30-35 min./lb.
rotated	up to 20		20-25 min./lb.
Hot Dogs	up to 20		10-15 min./lb.
BEEF			
Standing Rib Roast	6 lbs.	160° medium	18 min./lb.
Rolled Rib Roast	4 lbs.	140° rare	16 min./lb.
		160°medium	18 min./lb.
		170°well	20 min./lb.
Steaks	1-1/4 inch	medium	25 min. total
Hamburgers (9)	1/4 lb. each	medium-well	20-30 min. total
Beef Kebobs	6 skewers	medium	20-25 min. total
LAMB			
Leg of Lamb	4-1/2 to 7 lbs.	160° medium	22 min./lb.
SEAFOOD			
Salmon Steaks (In Basket)	4 steaks, 1-1/4 inch		20 min. total
Fish Fillets (In Basket)	3/4 inch		25min. total
Shrimp Kebobs	6 kebobs		25 min. total
Halibut Fillets (In Basket)	3/4 inch (breaded w/dill)		30 min. total
Baked Potato(s)	On Spit Rods		45 minutes

The LEAN
Rotisserie

The LEAN
Rotisserie

SALADS

The LEAN
Rotisserie

ROAST CHICKEN & BLACK BEAN SALAD
WITH CHIPOTLE LIME DRESSING

SERVES 4

2 (6 ounce) chicken breast halves, skin removed
1 large red bell pepper
Olive oil cooking spray
1 (14-1/2 ounce) can black beans, drained and rinsed
1 cup frozen corn, thawed
2 green onions, sliced
4 cups mixed lettuce greens

DRESSING:
1 tablespoon olive oil
2 tablespoons fresh lime juice
1 teaspoon honey
1 teaspoon minced Chipotle chilies in adobo sauce

Wash and dry the chicken breasts. Cut the red pepper in half and remove all seeds and membrane. Spray the Flat Standard Basket with the olive oil cooking spray as well as both sides of the chicken and peppers. Place both chicken and peppers in the basket leaving space between the pieces. Rotate for 35 to 40 minutes or until chicken is browned and cooked through. Remove and let chicken and peppers cool. Peel peppers and dice. Remove skin from chicken and dice meat. Toss peppers and chicken with black beans, corn and green onions. Cover and refrigerate until serving time.

At serving time, make the dressing by whisking all the ingredients together. Pour dressing over the chicken mixture and toss to coat. To serve, divide lettuce evenly among four serving plates and top with chicken mixture.

NUTRITIONAL ANALYSIS PER SERVING: 272 Calories, 47.2 g Carbohydrates, 10.5 g Protein, 5.8 g Fat, 5.4 mg Cholesterol, 315 mg Sodium

The LEAN
Rotisserie

TEQUILA CHICKEN SALAD

SERVES 6

MARINADE:
1/2 cup chopped onion
1/2 cup Tequila
1/4 cup fresh lime juice
1 tablespoon olive oil

3/4 cup fat-free mayonnaise
2 tablespoons toasted pine nuts
1 tablespoon chopped fresh cilantro
2 tablespoons Tequila
4 teaspoons fresh lime juice
1/4 teaspoon salt
1/8 teaspoon cayenne pepper
6 cups torn iceberg lettuce
2 medium tomatoes, each cut into 6 wedges
1-1/2 pounds skinless boneless chicken breast halves

For marinade combine onion, Tequila, lime juice and olive oil. Pound the chicken breasts to an even thickness of 1/2 inch. Add to the marinade and refrigerate 30 minutes, turning occasionally. Remove chicken from marinade and rotate in the Flat Standard Basket for 15 to 20 minutes or until chicken is cooked through. Remove and cool. Cut chicken into 1/2-inch pieces. Combine chicken, mayonnaise, pine nuts, cilantro, Tequila, lime juice, salt and cayenne in a bowl; stir well. Place 1 cup lettuce on each serving plate and top each with 2/3 cup chicken mixture and 2 tomato wedges.

NUTRITIONAL ANALYSIS PER SERVING: 234 Calories, 10.6 g Carbohydrates, 28.2 g Protein, 5.8 g Fat, 72 mg Cholesterol, 452 mg Sodium

CHICKEN & SPINACH SALAD WITH CHUTNEY DRESSING

SERVES 4

CHUTNEY DRESSING:
3/4 cup mango or peach chutney
2 tablespoons cider vinegar
1 tablespoon vegetable oil
1 teaspoon Dijon mustard
1 teaspoon honey
Salt and pepper to taste

2 (6 ounce) chicken breast halves, skin removed
8 large mushrooms, sliced
1 (11 ounce) can Mandarin oranges, drained
1 (7 ounce) can sliced water chestnuts, drained and rinsed
2 (6 ounce) bags washed baby spinach

To make the dressing, place all the ingredients in a jar and shake vigorously to combine. Chill up to 24 hours.

Wash and dry the chicken breasts. Measure out 2 tablespoons of the Chutney Dressing and brush on the chicken. Rotate the chicken in the Flat Standard Basket for 35 to 40 minutes or until chicken is browned and cooked through. Remove and let chicken cool. Remove skin and bones from chicken. Cut chicken across into 1/2-inch thick slices. Just before serving toss chicken with mushrooms, oranges, water chestnuts, and spinach in a large bowl. Add the dressing and toss lightly but thoroughly and serve immediately.

NUTRITIONAL ANALYSIS PER SERVING: 106 Calories, 6.5 g Carbohydrates, 11 g Protein, 4.4 g Fat, 22 mg Cholesterol, 352 mg Sodium

LEAN CHICKEN CAESAR SALAD
SERVES 6

4 slices French bread
Vegetable cooking spray
1/2 teaspoon garlic powder
6 (4 ounce) skinless boneless chicken breast halves
1/3 cup fresh lemon juice
1/4 cup red wine vinegar
1 tablespoon olive oil
1 teaspoon anchovy paste (optional)
1/4 teaspoon freshly ground pepper
1/4 teaspoon salt
5 cloves garlic
9 cups torn pieces Romaine lettuce
1/4 cup freshly grated Parmesan cheese

Trim crusts from bread and cut bread into 1-inch cubes. Arrange cubes on a baking pan. Spray with cooking spray and sprinkle with garlic powder; toss well. Bake at 350 degrees for 15 minutes or until lightly browned; set aside to cool. Trim chicken breasts and pound to an even thickness. Rotate in the Flat Standard Basket for 20 minutes or until chicken is cooked through. Cut chicken across into thin slices; set aside to cool.

Combine lemon juice, vinegar, olive oil, Anchovy paste, pepper, salt and garlic in blender and process until smooth. Add 1/4 cup dressing to chicken, tossing to coat. Place lettuce in large bowl and drizzle and toss with remaining dressing. Serve lettuce topped with chicken strips, grated cheese and croutons.

NUTRITIONAL ANALYSIS PER SERVING: 257 Calories, 10.8 g Carbohydrates, 33.7 g Protein, 7.9 g Fat, 85 mg Cholesterol, 303 mg Sodium

PASTA CHICKEN CAESAR SALAD

SERVES 8

4 (4 ounce) skinless boneless chicken breast halves
1/4 cup nonfat Caesar dressing
6 cups cooked penne pasta
4 cups thinly sliced Romaine lettuce
2 cups halved cherry tomatoes
1/2 cup thinly sliced fresh basil
1/2 cup chopped green onions
2/3 cup fat-free Caesar dressing
1 clove garlic, minced
1/4 cup chopped fresh parsley
1/2 cup crumbled Feta cheese

Pound chicken between two sheets of plastic wrap to an even thickness of 1/2 inch. Brush with 1/4 cup Caesar dressing and cook in the Flat Standard Basket for 20 minutes or until cooked through. Set aside to cool.

Toss pasta, lettuce, cherry tomatoes, basil, green onions, Caesar dressing and garlic together in a large serving bowl. Add the chicken and toss again. Serve sprinkled with parsley and Feta cheese.

NUTRITIONAL ANALYSIS PER SERVING: 362 Calories, 40.4 g Carbohydrates, 19.4 g Protein, 8.8 g Fat, 78 mg Cholesterol, 525 mg Sodium

The**LEAN**
Rotisserie

Triple Pepper Chicken Salad
Serves 4

1/2 teaspoon ground white pepper
1/2 teaspoon cayenne pepper
1/2 teaspoon ground black pepper
1/2 teaspoon garlic powder
4 (4 ounce) skinless boneless chicken breast halves
2 cups finely shredded lettuce
1 medium red bell pepper, diced
2 tablespoons low-fat mayonnaise
2 tablespoons plain low-fat yogurt
1 tablespoon prepared horseradish

Combine the peppers and garlic powder in a small bowl. Trim chicken and pound to an even thickness. Rub pepper mixture evenly into chicken; cover and refrigerate 8 hours.

Rotate chicken in the Flat Standard Basket for 20 minutes or until the chicken is cooked through. Remove chicken; cover and refrigerate 2 hours. Slice chicken across grain into 1/2-inch strips. Stir together mayonnaise, yogurt and horseradish to make dressing.

Combine lettuce and red pepper and divide evenly among four serving plates. Arrange chicken over salad mixture. Top each salad with 1 tablespoon of the dressing.

NUTRITIONAL ANALYSIS PER SERVING: 181 Calories, 4.6 g Carbohydrates, 27 g Protein, 5.5 g Fat, 73 mg Cholesterol, 131 mg Sodium

CUMIN CHICKEN SALAD WITH ORANGE SESAME DRESSING

SERVES 4

4 (4 ounce) skinless boneless chicken breast halves
1 tablespoon ground cumin
1 teaspoon paprika
1/8 teaspoon salt
1/8 teaspoon freshly ground pepper
2 teaspoons vegetable oil
6 cups mixed salad greens
3 tablespoons white wine vinegar
3 tablespoons orange marmalade
2 tablespoons low-sodium soy sauce
1 teaspoon Oriental sesame oil
4 lemon wedges

Trim chicken and pound to an even thickness. Combine cumin, paprika, salt and pepper on a plate. Brush chicken with oil and coat with spices. Rotate chicken in the Flat Standard Basket for 20 minutes or until cooked through.

Place salad greens in a large bowl. To make dressing, combine vinegar, marmalade, soy sauce and sesame oil; whisk until blended. Pour over greens; toss well to coat. Divide evenly among four plates. Cut each chicken across in thin slices and arrange on top of lettuce. Serve with lemon wedges.

NUTRITIONAL ANALYSIS PER SERVING: 226 Calories, 12.5 g Carbohydrates, 28.3 g Protein, 7.3 g Fat, 72 mg Cholesterol, 347 mg Sodium

BUFFALO CHICKEN SALAD
SERVES 6

1 tablespoon paprika
1-1/2 tablespoons olive oil
2 tablespoons hot sauce
6 (4 ounce) skinless boneless chicken breast halves
1 large carrot
1 celery stalk
3 cups cubed red potatoes
6 cups shredded Romaine lettuce
2 cups cherry tomato halves

BLUE CHEESE-BUTTERMILK DRESSING:
1/2 cup low-fat buttermilk
1/2 cup plain fat-free yogurt
3 tablespoons white wine vinegar
1 teaspoon sugar
1/2 teaspoon salt
1/2 teaspoon freshly ground pepper
1/2 cup thinly sliced green onions
1/2 cup (2 ounces) crumbled Blue cheese

Combine paprika, olive oil and hot sauce in a shallow dish. Trim chicken and pound to an even thickness. Place chicken in dish, turning to coat with sauce. Cover and refrigerate for 30 to 60 minutes.

Rotate in the Flat Standard Basket for 20 minutes or until chicken is cooked through.

Cut chicken across the grain into thin slices. Cut carrot and celery lengthwise into 12 thin strips using a vegetable peeler. Place strips in a bowl of ice water for 30 minutes. Cook potatoes until tender, about 15 minutes; drain and cool.

To make dressing, whisk buttermilk, yogurt, vinegar, sugar, salt and pepper together until blended. Stir in green onion and cheese.

Divide lettuce evenly between six plates. Top with potato, carrot and celery, chicken and tomato halves. Serve with dressing, about 1/4 cup per serving.

NUTRITIONAL ANALYSIS PER SERVING: 378 Calories, 30.7 g Carbohydrates, 37.6 g Protein, 11.4 g Fat, 87 mg Cholesterol, 827 mg Sodium

CRANBERRY TURKEY SALAD

SERVES 6

CRANBERRY DRESSING:
1 cup jellied cranberry sauce
2 shallots, chopped
2 tablespoons raspberry vinegar
2 tablespoons fresh orange juice
4 tablespoons olive oil

3 cups leftover roast turkey, cubed
3 oranges, peeled and sliced
2 celery stalks, sliced thin
1/2 cup thinly sliced red onion
12 cups mixed salad greens

To make the dressing, combine all ingredients in a food processor or blender and puree. Cover and refrigerate up to 3 days.

Divide lettuce evenly among six plates. Top with turkey, oranges, celery, and onion. Drizzle dressing over all and serve immediately.

NUTRITIONAL ANALYSIS PER SERVING: 353 Calories, 34.1 g Carbohydrates, 21.4 g Protein, 17 g Fat, 64 mg Cholesterol, 94 mg Sodium

SHRIMP AND ASPARAGUS PASTA SALAD

SERVES 6

6 ounces bow-tie pasta
1/2 pound fresh asparagus spears
1/2 cup plain low-fat yogurt
1/3 cup reduced fat creamy Italian salad dressing
1 clove garlic, minced
2 pounds large raw shrimp, peeled and deveined
Vegetable cooking spray
12 cherry tomatoes, halved
1 medium cucumber, sliced
1 cup shredded carrot
2 green onions, chopped

Cook the pasta in boiling water just until tender, about 9 minutes. Drain and rinse in cold water. Snap off tough ends of asparagus and cut into 1-inch pieces. Cook in the microwave oven on HIGH power in a covered dish with 2 tablespoons water for 2 minutes. Rinse in cold water and add to pasta.

To make dressing, whisk together the yogurt, salad dressing and garlic. Stir into pasta and asparagus; cover and refrigerate.

Thread shrimp on kebob skewers, spray with vegetable cooking spray and rotate for 15 minutes or until shrimp are cooked through. Add shrimp to pasta along with tomatoes, cucumber, carrot and onions. Serve immediately or cover and chill until serving time.

NUTRITIONAL ANALYSIS PER SERVING: 252 Calories, 15.7 g Carbohydrates, 13.4 g Protein, 0.9 g Fat, 86 mg Cholesterol, 152 mg Sodium

The LEAN
Rotisserie

Spicy Asian Shrimp Salad with Peanut Dressing

Serves 6

4-1/2 cups finely shredded red cabbage
3 cups bean sprouts
2-1/2 cups shredded carrots
1/2 pound snow peas, cut into julienne strips
1 medium red bell pepper, cut into julienne strips
1/4 cup diagonally sliced green onions
2 pounds large raw shrimp, shelled and deveined
Vegetable cooking spray

Peanut Sauce:
1/2 cup soft tofu
1/3 cup canned chicken broth
1/4 cup low-sodium soy sauce
3 tablespoons balsamic vinegar
3 tablespoons dry sherry
3 tablespoons creamy peanut butter
2 cloves garlic, minced
1 tablespoon plus 1-1/2 teaspoons sugar
1 tablespoon minced fresh ginger root
1 teaspoon Oriental sesame oil
1/2 teaspoon crushed red pepper flakes

Combine cabbage, bean sprouts, carrots, snow peas, red pepper and green onions in a large bowl. Make the Peanut Sauce by combining all ingredients in the blender or food processor and pureeing until smooth. Spoon Peanut Sauce over cabbage mixture and toss gently. Set aside.

Thread Shrimp on the kebob skewers and spray with vegetable cooking spray. Rotate shrimp for 15 minutes or until cooked through. Top cabbage salad with shrimp and serve immediately

NUTRITIONAL ANALYSIS PER SERVING: 270 Calories, 22.8 g Carbohydrates, 29.2 g Protein, 7.2 g Fat, 196 mg Cholesterol, 696 mg Sodium

The **LEAN** Rotisserie

CILANTRO PESTO SHRIMP PASTA SALAD

SERVES 6

PESTO:
1/4 cup chopped garlic
1/2 cup chopped fresh ginger root
1-1/2 cups chopped cilantro
1 teaspoon ground nutmeg
1 teaspoon five spice powder
1 tablespoon brown sugar
3 tablespoons low-sodium soy sauce
2 tablespoons Spanish sherry or white wine vinegar
2 tablespoons water
2 tablespoons vegetable oil

SALAD:
8 ounces spaghetti, cooked
2 pounds raw shrimp, shelled and deveined
1 red bell pepper, cut into thin strips
1/2 cup shredded carrots
2 tablespoons cilantro leaves

To make the pesto, combine all of the ingredients in a food processor or blender and puree to a smooth paste.

Cook the spaghetti; then drain and rinse in cold water.

Immediately stir 3 tablespoons of the pesto into the pasta and set aside. Stir the remaining pesto into the shrimp. Cover and refrigerate both for 1 to 2 hours.

Remove pasta and shrimp from refrigerator. Thread the shrimp on the kebob skewers and rotate 15 minutes or until shrimp are cooked through and turn bright orange in color. Toss with pasta, red bell pepper and carrots. Sprinkle with cilantro and serve.

NUTRITIONAL ANALYSIS PER SERVING: 398 Calories, 41.5 g Carbohydrates, 38.4 g Protein, 8.4 g Fat, 230 mg Cholesterol, 494 mg Sodium

SCALLOP AND CABBAGE SALAD

SERVES 4

1-1/2 pounds sea scallops
Vegetable cooking spray
2 teaspoons chili powder
1 teaspoon freshly ground pepper
8 cups coarsely chopped Chinese Napa cabbage
2 cups red bell pepper strips
1/2 cup finely chopped fresh basil
1/2 cup minced fresh cilantro
1/3 cup finely chopped fresh mint

DRESSING:
1/2 cup fresh lime juice
3 tablespoons sugar
2 tablespoons finely chopped dry-roasted peanuts
2 tablespoons fish sauce,
or 1 tablespoon low-sodium soy sauce
1 teaspoon minced fresh ginger root
2 cloves garlic, minced
1 tablespoon minced serrano chili (optional)

Spray scallops with vegetable cooking spray and sprinkle with chili powder and pepper. Thread on kebob skewers and rotate 15 minutes or until scallops are opaque.

To make dressing, whisk together all ingredients and set aside.

Combine the cabbage, pepper strips, basil, cilantro and mint in a large bowl. Add the dressing and toss well.

Divide cabbage evenly among four serving plates. Top with warm scallops and serve immediately.

NUTRITIONAL ANALYSIS PER SERVING: 267 Calories, 25.9 g Carbohydrates, 33.2 g Protein, 4.4 g Fat, 56 mg Cholesterol, 1403 mg Sodium

The LEAN Rotisserie

SESAME ORANGE PORK SALAD

SERVES 4

3/4 cup fresh orange juice
1/4 cup low-sodium teriyaki sauce
1 tablespoon rice vinegar
1 tablespoon mirin (sweet rice wine)
2 teaspoons hoisin sauce
1 teaspoon Oriental sesame oil
1 clove garlic, minced
3 tablespoons brown sugar
2 tablespoons bourbon
1/4 teaspoon crushed red pepper flakes
1 1-pound pork tenderloin
8 cups mixed salad greens
1/2 cup sliced red onion
1 (11 ounce) can mandarin oranges, drained
1 (8 ounce) can sliced water chestnuts, rinsed and drained
1 large red bell pepper, sliced into rings
2 tablespoons toasted sesame seeds

To make dressing, combine 1/2 cup plus 2 tablespoons orange juice, 2 tablespoons teriyaki sauce, vinegar, and mirin, hoisin, sesame oil and garlic in a small bowl; stir well. Cover and chill.

Combine remaining orange juice and teriyaki sauce with brown sugar, bourbon and red pepper flakes in a large bowl.

Trim the fat and silverskin from the pork tenderloin. Cut lengthwise down the center of the tenderloin but not all the way through. Lay open and press to flatten slightly. Add to marinade and turn to coat. Cover and refrigerate for 30 minutes and up to 4 hours.

Rotate pork in the Flat Standard Basket for 15 minutes or until just cooked through. Slice across into 1/2 inch thick strips.

Divide salad greens, onion, orange, water chestnuts and bell pepper evenly among four plates. Top with pork slices. Drizzle with reserved orange juice dressing over all. Sprinkle with sesame seeds and serve.

NUTRITIONAL ANALYSIS PER SERVING: 322 Calories, 37.3 g Carbohydrates, 28 g Protein, 6.8 g Fat, 74 mg Cholesterol, 382 mg Sodium

The LEAN
Rotisserie

WARM FAJITA STEAK SALAD

SERVES 6

1 pound lean top sirloin or flank steak
1/4 cup dry red wine
1/4 cup fresh lime juice
1/2 teaspoon garlic powder
1/2 teaspoon cumin
2 cups seeded, diced fresh tomato
1 small green or yellow bell pepper, diced
1 jalapeno chili, seeded and diced
2 tablespoons diced purple onion
1 tablespoon minced fresh cilantro
1 tablespoon balsamic vinegar
6 cups torn romaine lettuce
1/2 cup (2 ounces) shredded extra-sharp cheddar cheese

Trim fat from steak and place in a large shallow dish. Combine red wine, lime juice, garlic powder and cumin and pour over steak. Cover and marinate in refrigerator 24 hours, turning steak occasionally.

To make salsa combine tomato, bell pepper, chili, onion and cilantro in a medium bowl. Toss in the vinegar. Set aside.

Remove steak from marinade and rotate in the Flat Standard Basket 15 minutes for medium rare. Cut steak diagonally across grain into thin slices. Combine lettuce, steak and cheese in a large bowl; toss gently. Divide evenly among six serving plates and top each with 1/3 cup salsa. Serve warm.

NUTRITIONAL ANALYSIS PER SERVING: 210 Calories, 5.7 g Carbohydrates, 18.8 g Protein, 12.2 g Fat, 51 mg Cholesterol, 117 mg Sodium

ASIAN BEEF SALAD
SERVES 4

1 pound lean top sirloin or flank steak
1/4 teaspoon salt
1/8 teaspoon freshly ground pepper
1/4 cup seasoned rice vinegar
1/4 cup fresh lime juice
1 tablespoon low-sodium soy sauce
1 teaspoon minced fresh ginger root
1/8 teaspoon crushed red pepper flakes
6 cups chopped romaine lettuce
1-1/2 cups bean sprouts
1/2 cup red bell pepper strips

Trim fat from steak. Sprinkle both sides with salt and pepper. Rotate steak in Flat Standard Basket for 15 minutes for medium rare. Cut steak across grain into thin slices about 2 inches long.

Combine vinegar, lime juice, soy sauce, ginger and red pepper flakes in a small bowl. Toss lettuce with bean sprouts, red pepper and steak. Drizzle vinaigrette over salad; toss to coat and serve.

NUTRITIONAL ANALYSIS PER SERVING: 245 Calories, 7.2 g Carbohydrates, 24.3 g Protein, 13.2 g Fat, 60 mg Cholesterol, 325 mg Sodium

The LEAN
Rotisserie

The LEAN Rotisserie

CHICKEN

The LEAN
Rotisserie

GARLIC & HERB ROAST CHICKEN

SERVES 4

1 3-1/2 to 4 pound whole chicken
5 cloves garlic, minced
1 tablespoon dried basil
1 tablespoon dried oregano
1-1/2 teaspoons dried thyme
1-1/2 teaspoons dried rosemary
1-1/2 teaspoons rubbed sage
1 teaspoon salt
1/2 teaspoon freshly ground pepper

Wash the chicken and dry thoroughly, inside and out. Loosen the skin across the breast and then down around the leg and thigh using a chopstick or your fingers, being careful not to tear the skin. In a small bowl or with a mortar and pestle combine the garlic, herbs, salt and pepper to form a moist paste. Work the rub under the skin and onto the meat of the breasts, legs and thighs and then all over the outside skin as well. Season the inside cavity with any remaining rub.

Using an elastic food tie, truss the chicken. Rotate the chicken on the spit rods for 55 to 60 minutes or until the internal temperature reaches 170 degrees on the instant thermometer inserted in the thigh meat. Remove the chicken skin and cut into serving pieces before serving.

Tip: If you are roasting two chickens at the same time, skewer them side by side on the spit rods and increase the cooking time to 1-1/2 hours.

NUTRITIONAL ANALYSIS PER SERVING: 325 Calories, 3.4 g Carbohydrates, 58.5 g Protein, 7.3 g Fat, 191 mg Cholesterol, 739 mg Sodium

The LEAN
Rotisserie

RASPBERRY-ORANGE
ROAST CHICKEN
SERVES 4

1 3-1/2 to 4 pound chicken
2 tablespoons olive oil
1/2 cup low-sugar orange marmalade
1/4 cup raspberry vinegar
1/2 teaspoon dried thyme

Wash the chicken and dry thoroughly, inside and out. Loosen the skin across the breast and then down around the leg and thigh using a chopstick or your fingers, being careful not to tear the skin.

Combine the olive oil, marmalade, vinegar and thyme in a small saucepan. Cook over medium heat until heated and smooth, stirring often. Divide the sauce in half. Set half aside to serve with the chicken. Work the remaining sauce under the skin and onto the meat of the breasts, legs and thighs and then all over the outside skin as well.

Using an elastic food tie, truss the chicken. Rotate the chicken on the spit rods for 55 to 60 minutes or until the internal temperature reaches 170 degrees on the instant thermometer inserted in the thigh meat. Remove the chicken skin and cut into serving pieces before serving with reserved sauce.

NUTRITIONAL ANALYSIS PER SERVING: 354 Calories, 27.5 g Carbohydrates, 38 g Protein, 13.9 g Fat, 223 mg Cholesterol, 254 mg Sodium

ORANGE-SOY MARINATED ROAST CHICKEN

SERVES 4

1/4 cup low-sodium soy sauce
1/4 cup orange juice concentrate
2 tablespoons fresh lemon juice
2 tablespoons ketchup
2 cloves garlic, minced
1 3-1/2 to 4 pound whole chicken

Stir together the soy sauce, orange juice concentrate, lemon juice, ketchup and garlic. Wash the chicken and dry thoroughly, inside and out. Loosen the skin across the breast and then down around the leg and thigh using a chopstick or your fingers, being careful not to tear the skin.

Work the sauce under the skin and over the meat of the breasts, legs and thighs and then all over the outside skin as well.

Using an elastic food tie, truss the chicken. Rotate the chicken on the spit rods for 55 to 60 minutes or until the internal temperature reaches 170 degrees on the instant thermometer inserted in the thigh meat. Remove the chicken skin and cut into serving pieces before serving.

NUTRITIONAL ANALYSIS PER SERVING: 334 Calories, 5.4 g Carbohydrates, 58.9 g Protein, 7 g Fat, 191 mg Cholesterol, 777 mg Sodium

The LEAN
Rotisserie

Tangerine-Flavored Roast Chicken

Serves 4

2 tablespoons dry bread crumbs
1 teaspoon grated tangerine or orange zest
2 tablespoons fresh tangerine or orange juice
2 tablespoons minced fresh ginger root
1 tablespoon low-sodium soy sauce
1 tablespoon honey
1 teaspoon Oriental sesame oil
1 3-1/2 pound whole chicken

In a small bowl combine the bread crumbs, tangerine zest and juice, ginger, soy sauce, honey and sesame oil. Wash and pat dry the chicken. Loosen the skin across the breast and then down around the leg and thigh using a chopstick or your fingers, being careful not to tear the skin.

Work the sauce under the skin and over the meat of the breasts, legs and thighs and then all over the outside skin as well.

Using an elastic food tie, truss the chicken. Rotate the chicken on the spit rods for 55 to 60 minutes or until the internal temperature reaches 170 degrees on the instant thermometer inserted in the thigh meat. Remove the chicken skin and cut into serving pieces before serving.

NUTRITIONAL ANALYSIS PER SERVING: 397 Calories, 8.5 g Carbohydrates, 74.1 g Protein, 5.3 g Fat, 184 mg Cholesterol, 352 mg Sodium

BALSAMIC GINGER ROAST CHICKEN

SERVES 4

2 tablespoons grainy mustard
1/4 cup balsamic vinegar
2 tablespoons low-sodium soy sauce
3 cloves garlic, minced
2 teaspoons minced fresh ginger root
1/4 teaspoon freshly ground pepper
1 3-1/2 pound whole chicken

In a small bowl combine the mustard, vinegar, soy sauce, garlic, ginger and pepper. Wash and pat dry the chicken. Loosen the skin across the breast and then down around the leg and thigh using a chopstick or your fingers, being careful not to tear the skin.

Work the marinade under the skin and over the meat of the breasts, legs and thighs and then all over the outside skin as well. Cover and refrigerate at least 1 hour and up to 8 hours.

Using an elastic food tie, truss the chicken. Rotate the chicken on the spit rods for 55 to 60 minutes or until the internal temperature reaches 170 degrees on the instant thermometer inserted in the thigh meat. Remove the chicken skin and cut into serving pieces before serving.

NUTRITIONAL ANALYSIS PER SERVING: 365 Calories, 2.9 g Carbohydrates, 74.3 g Protein, 4.3 g Fat, 184 mg Cholesterol, 543 mg Sodium

The LEAN
Rotisserie

JAMAICAN JERK ROAST CHICKEN

SERVES 4

1/4 cup plain nonfat yogurt
1 teaspoon sugar
1 teaspoon ground allspice
1/2 teaspoon salt
1/2 teaspoon dried thyme
1/2 teaspoon cayenne pepper
1/4 teaspoon ground mace
1/4 teaspoon ground nutmeg
1/4 teaspoon freshly ground pepper
1 3-1/2 pound chicken

In a small bowl combine the yogurt, sugar and spices. Wash and pat dry the chicken. Loosen the skin across the breast and then down around the leg and thigh using a chopstick or your fingers, being careful not to tear the skin.

Work the sauce under the skin and over the meat of the breasts, legs and thighs and then all over the outside skin as well.

Using an elastic food tie, truss the chicken. Rotate the chicken on the spit rods for 55 to 60 minutes or until the internal temperature reaches 170 degrees on the instant thermometer inserted in the thigh meat. Remove the chicken skin and cut into serving pieces before serving.

NUTRITIONAL ANALYSIS PER SERVING: 366 Calories, 0.3 g Carbohydrates, 74.3 g Protein, 4.2 g Fat, 185 mg Cholesterol, 485 mg Sodium

MOROCCAN SPICED ROAST CHICKEN

SERVES 4

1/2 cup chopped fresh parsley
1/2 cup chopped fresh cilantro or mint
1 tablespoon ground cinnamon
1 tablespoon ground ginger
1 tablespoon paprika
1 teaspoon freshly ground pepper
1/2 teaspoon ground cumin
1/2 teaspoon ground thyme
1/2 teaspoon cayenne pepper
1 3-1/2 pound chicken

Combine parsley, cilantro or mint or half each, spices and herbs in the food processor and puree to a smooth paste.

Wash and pat dry the chicken. Loosen the skin across the breast and then down around the leg and thigh using a chopstick or your fingers, being careful not to tear the skin. Work the paste under the skin and over the meat of the breasts, legs and thighs and then all over the outside skin as well.

Using an elastic food tie, truss the chicken. Rotate the chicken on the spit rods for 55 to 60 minutes or until the internal temperature reaches 170 degrees on the instant thermometer inserted in the thigh meat. Remove the chicken skin and cut into serving pieces before serving.

NUTRITIONAL ANALYSIS PER SERVING: 380 Calories, 6.3 g Carbohydrates, 75 g Protein, 4.7 g Fat, 184 mg Cholesterol, 221 mg Sodium

The LEAN
Rotisserie

CHUTNEY & CURRY
ROAST CHICKEN

SERVES 4

1/2 cup mango chutney
1 teaspoon curry power
1 3-1/2 pound whole chicken

In a small bowl combine the chutney and curry powder. Wash and pat dry the chicken. Loosen the skin across the breast and then down around the leg and thigh using a chopstick or your fingers, being careful not to tear the skin. Work the sauce under the skin and over the meat of the breasts, legs and thighs and then all over the outside skin as well.

Using an elastic food tie, truss the chicken. Rotate the chicken on the spit rods for 55 to 60 minutes or until the internal temperature reaches 170 degrees on the instant thermometer inserted in the thigh meat. Remove the chicken skin and cut into serving pieces before serving.

NUTRITIONAL ANALYSIS PER SERVING: 412 Calories, 15.9 g Carbohydrates, 74 g Protein, 4.2 g Fat, 184 mg Cholesterol, 295 mg Sodium

LOW-FAT CHICKEN PARMESAN

SERVES 4

3 pounds cut-up chicken pieces (breasts and/or thighs)
Salt and pepper to taste
1/4 cup fine dry bread crumbs
1/4 cup freshly grated Parmesan cheese
1/2 teaspoon dried parsley flakes
1/4 teaspoon dried oregano
1/2 teaspoon paprika
3 egg whites, lightly beaten

Remove skin from chicken pieces; wash and pat dry. Season chicken with salt and pepper. In a shallow bowl or pie plate toss together the bread crumbs, cheese, parsley, oregano and paprika.

Dip the chicken in the beaten egg whites and then coat with the bread crumbs. Rotate the chicken in the Flat Standard Basket for 45 minutes or until lightly browned and cooked through.

NUTRITIONAL ANALYSIS PER SERVING: 166 Calories, 5.4 g Carbohydrates, 24.8 g Protein, 4.3 g Fat, 676 mg Cholesterol, 383 mg Sodium

The LEAN Rotisserie

CRUSTY BBQ CHICKEN BREASTS

SERVES 6

2 tablespoons paprika
1-1/2 teaspoons ground cumin
1-1/2 teaspoons chili powder
1-1/2 teaspoons brown sugar
1/2 teaspoon garlic powder
1/2 teaspoon salt
1/4 teaspoon cayenne pepper
1/4 teaspoon freshly ground pepper
6 (6 ounce) chicken breast halves
Olive oil cooking spray

To make the rub, toss the paprika, cumin, chili powder, sugar, garlic powder, salt, cayenne and pepper together in a small bowl. Remove the skin from the breasts and rub about one tablespoon of the seasoning all over each piece of chicken.

Spray the chicken lightly with the olive oil cooking spray. Rotate the chicken in the Flat Standard Basket for 45 minutes or until lightly browned and cooked through.

Tip: Any leftover chicken is delicious when shredded and added to a salad or wrapped in a tortilla with lettuce and tomato.

NUTRITIONAL ANALYSIS PER SERVING: 100 Calories, 4.3 g Carbohydrates, 27.4 g Protein, 2.25 g Fat, 66.7 mg Cholesterol, 378 mg Sodium

LEMON GARLIC CHICKEN WITH BLOND BBQ SAUCE

SERVES 4

4 chicken drumsticks (about 1 pound)
4 chicken thighs (about 1 pound)
1/3 cup fresh lemon juice
3 tablespoons Dijon mustard
1/4 teaspoon garlic powder
2 tablespoons light mayonnaise
2 tablespoons barbecue sauce
1 teaspoon chili powder
1/4 teaspoon paprika
3/4 cup Italian seasoned bread crumbs
1/4 cup freshly grated Parmesan cheese

Remove skin and trim excess fat from chicken pieces. Combine lemon juice, mustard and garlic powder in a large bowl. Remove 2 tablespoons and reserve. Add chicken to large bowl, turning to coat. Cover and refrigerate 30 minutes.

Combine reserved 2 tablespoons lemon mixture with mayonnaise, barbecue sauce, chili powder and paprika. Cover and chill.

Combine bread crumbs and Parmesan. Remove chicken from bowl and dredge in crumbs. Rotate in the Flat Standard Basket for 45 to 50 minutes or until cooked through. Serve with sauce.

NUTRITIONAL ANALYSIS PER SERVING: 301 Calories, 20.3 g Carbohydrates, 27 g Protein, 11.7 g Fat, 80 mg Cholesterol, 1.22 mg Sodium

The**LEAN**
Rotisserie

MARINATED CHICKEN PIECES

SERVES 4

1/2 cup fresh orange juice
1/4 cup fresh lemon juice
1 teaspoon Dijon mustard
1 teaspoon Worcestershire sauce
1 tablespoon vegetable oil
2 cloves garlic, minced
1/4 cup chopped fresh parsley
1 teaspoon dried oregano
1/2 teaspoon salt
1/4 teaspoon freshly ground pepper
2 chicken breasts, skin removed
2 chicken thighs, skin removed

Combine orange juice, lemon juice, mustard and Worcestershire in a medium mixing bowl. Whisk in oil, garlic, parsley, oregano, salt and pepper. Wash and pat dry chicken pieces and add to marinade. Cover and refrigerate 3 to 4 hours.

Remove chicken from marinade and rotate in the Flat Standard Basket for 45 minutes or until cooked through and browned.

NUTRITIONAL ANALYSIS PER SERVING: 176 Calories, 5.5 g Carbohydrates, 26.4g Protein, 5 g Fat, 65 mg Cholesterol, 372 mg Sodium

MUSTARD CRUSTED
CHICKEN BREASTS
SERVES 4

2 tablespoons low-fat mayonnaise
2 tablespoons Dijon mustard
1/4 cup wheat germ
1/3 cup fine, dry bread crumbs
1/2 teaspoon dried thyme
1/4 teaspoon salt
4 (6 ounce) chicken breast halves, skin removed

Stir together the mayonnaise and mustard. Combine the wheat germ, bread crumbs, thyme, and salt on a plate. Brush the chicken with the mustard-mayonnaise mixture and then coat with the wheat germ mixture.

Rotate the chicken in the Flat Standard Basket for 45 minutes or until lightly browned and cooked through.

NUTRITIONAL ANALYSIS PER SERVING: 206 Calories, 10 g Carbohydrates, 29.9 g Protein, 5.2 g Fat, 69 mg Cholesterol, 435 mg Sodium

The LEAN
Rotisserie

LIGHT AND NUTTY CHICKEN BREASTS

SERVES 6

1/4 cup honey
2 tablespoons Dijon mustard
3/4 teaspoon paprika
1/8 teaspoon garlic powder
1 cup finely crushed cornflakes
1/2 cup finely chopped pecans
6 (6 ounce) chicken breast halves, skin removed
Salt and pepper

In a small bowl combine the honey, mustard, paprika and garlic powder. Toss together the cornflakes and pecans in a shallow dish.

Wash and pat dry chicken. Sprinkle chicken lightly with salt and pepper. Brush both sides of chicken with honey mixture and dredge in the cornflake mixture.

Rotate the chicken in the Flat Standard Basket for 45 minutes or until cooked through and crispy.

NUTRITIONAL ANALYSIS PER SERVING: 198 Calories, 17 g Carbohydrates, 22 g Protein, 4.6 g Fat, 53 mg Cholesterol, 170 mg Sodium

CORNFLAKE CRISPY CHICKEN THIGHS

SERVES 8

1 cup cornflake crumbs
1 teaspoon paprika
1/2 teaspoon onion powder
1/2 teaspoon dried oregano
1/2 teaspoon dry mustard
1/2 cup evaporated skimmed milk
8 (6 ounce) chicken thighs, skin removed

Combine crumbs, paprika, onion powder, oregano and dry mustard in a shallow dish; stir well. Pour milk into a small shallow bowl. Dip each chicken thigh in milk and dredge in corn flake mixture. Rotate chicken in the Flat Standard Basket for 45 minutes or until chicken is cooked through.

NUTRITIONAL ANALYSIS PER SERVING: 118 Calories, 9.9 g Carbohydrates, 13.3 g Protein, 2.5 g Fat, 49 mg Cholesterol, 155 mg Sodium

RANCH DRESSING CHICKEN PIECES

SERVES 4

4 chicken thigh and leg quarters, skin removed
1 cup nonfat Ranch Dressing

Toss chicken with Ranch Dressing. Cover and refrigerate for 1 to 4 hours. Rotate in the Flat Standard Basket for 50 minutes or until chicken is cooked through and browned.

NUTRITIONAL ANALYSIS PER SERVING: 322 Calories, 12 g Carbohydrates, 43 g Protein, 9.3 g Fat, 175 mg Cholesterol, 785 mg Sodium

The LEAN
Rotisserie

GINGER MOLASSES CHICKEN THIGHS

SERVES 8

8 (6 ounce) chicken thighs, skin removed
1/2 cup low-sodium soy sauce
1/4 cup molasses
1 tablespoon olive oil
1 teaspoon ground ginger

Wash chicken and pat dry and place in a shallow dish. Whisk together remaining ingredients and pour over chicken, turning to coat. Cover and refrigerate 4 hours.

Remove chicken from marinade and rotate in the Flat Standard Basket for 45 to 50 minutes or until chicken is cooked through and browned.

NUTRITIONAL ANALYSIS PER SERVING: 137 Calories, 8.5 g Carbohydrates, 15.3 g Protein, 4.6 g Fat, 61 mg Cholesterol, 551 mg Sodium

SESAME PINEAPPLE CHICKEN
SERVES 4

1 (8 ounce) can unsweetened pineapple slices, undrained
1 tablespoon toasted sesame seeds
3 tablespoons honey
1/4 teaspoon rubbed sage
4 (6 ounce) chicken breast halves, skin removed

Drain pineapple, reserving 3 tablespoons juice. Combine juice with sesame seeds, honey and sage in a flat dish. Add the chicken to the sauce, turning to coat. Reserve some of the sauce.

Place the chicken breasts in the Flat Standard Basket and top each with a slice of pineapple. Brush with the sauce. Rotate for 45 minutes or until the chicken is cooked through and golden, brushing with the reserved sauce once or twice toward the end.

NUTRITIONAL ANALYSIS PER SERVING: 240 Calories, 19.9 g Carbohydrates, 29.2 g Protein, 7.6 g Fat, 78 mg Cholesterol, 70 mg Sodium

The LEAN Rotisserie

ZESTY DIJON CHICKEN BREASTS

SERVES 6

6 (6 ounce) chicken breasts, skin removed
1/2 cup balsamic vinegar
1/4 cup Dijon mustard
1 tablespoon olive oil
1/4 teaspoon freshly ground pepper
1 clove garlic, minced

Wash and pat dry chicken breasts and place in a shallow dish. Whisk together remaining ingredients and pour over chicken, tossing to coat. Cover and refrigerate for up to 4 hours.

Remove chicken from marinade and rotate in the Flat Standard Basket for 45 minutes or until chicken is cooked through.

NUTRITIONAL ANALYSIS PER SERVING: 181 Calories, 2 g Carbohydrates, 31.9 g Protein, 4.4 g Fat, 79 mg Cholesterol, 214 mg Sodium

LEAN AND SPICY ROAST CHICKEN

SERVES 4

1 3 -1/2 pound whole chicken
2 tablespoons paprika
2 teaspoons chili powder
2 teaspoons sugar
2 teaspoons freshly ground black pepper
1 teaspoon salt
1 teaspoon garlic powder
1 teaspoon onion powder
1/2 teaspoon cayenne pepper

Wash the chicken and dry thoroughly, inside and out. Loosen the skin across the breast and then down around the leg and thigh using a chopstick or your fingers, being careful not to tear the skin. Combine the remaining ingredients to form the rub in a small bowl. Work the rub under the skin and onto the meat of the breasts, legs and thighs and then all over the outside skin as well. Season the inside cavity with any remaining rub.

Using an elastic food tie, truss the chicken. Rotate the chicken on the spit rods for 55 to 60 minutes or until the internal temperature reaches 170 degrees on the instant thermometer inserted in the thigh meat. Remove the chicken skin and cut into serving pieces before serving.

Tip: If you are roasting two chickens at the same time, skewer them side by side on the spit rods and increase the cooking time to 1-1/2 hours.

NUTRITIONAL ANALYSIS PER SERVING: 322 Calories, 12 g Carbohydrates, 43 g Protein, 9.3 g Fat, 175 mg Cholesterol, 785 mg Sodium

The LEAN Rotisserie

Zippy Hoisin Chicken Pieces

Serves 4

3 tablespoons Hoisin sauce
1 teaspoon chili paste with garlic
1/3 cup soy sauce
1 tablespoon honey
1 teaspoon Oriental sesame oil
2 tablespoons minced fresh ginger root
1/4 cup orange marmalade
4 chicken thigh and leg quarters, skin removed

Combine the hoisin sauce with chili paste, soy sauce, honey, sesame oil and ginger in a large bowl. Whisk in the marmalade. Wash and pat dry the chicken and add to the marinade. Cover and refrigerate 30 minutes to 4 hours.

Rotate chicken in the Flat Standard Basket for 50 minutes or until the chicken is cooked through and browned.

NUTRITIONAL ANALYSIS PER SERVING: 371 Calories, 37.4 g Carbohydrates, 22.5 g Protein, 11.1 g Fat, 175 mg Cholesterol

SESAME PLUM SAUCE CHICKEN
SERVES 6

6 (6 ounce) chicken breast halves, skin removed
2/3 cup Oriental plum sauce
2 teaspoons Hoisin sauce
2 tablespoons dry sherry
1 tablespoon low-sodium soy sauce
1 teaspoon Oriental sesame oil
1 tablespoon minced fresh ginger root
2 cloves garlic, minced
1/4 cup chopped cilantro
1/2 teaspoon crushed red pepper flakes

Wash chicken and pat dry; place in a large bowl. Combine plum sauce, Hoisin, sherry, soy sauce and sesame oil. Stir in ginger, garlic, cilantro, and red pepper flakes. Pour over chicken; cover and refrigerate for 4 to 6 hours.

Remove chicken from marinade and rotate in the Flat Standard Basket for 45 minutes or until cooked through and browned.

NUTRITIONAL ANALYSIS PER SERVING: 189 Calories, 6.1 g Carbohydrates, 32 g Protein, 2.8 g Fat, 79 mg Cholesterol, 355 mg Sodium

CHICKEN WITH LEMON
AND FRESH HERBS
SERVES 6

2 teaspoons grated lemon zest
1/2 cup fresh lemon juice
2 tablespoons olive oil
2 tablespoons water
1/4 cup minced fresh basil
2 teaspoons minced fresh thyme
1 teaspoon minced fresh rosemary
1/4 teaspoon freshly ground pepper
2 cloves garlic, minced
6 (6 ounce) chicken breast halves, skin removed

Combine the lemon zest and juice, olive oil, water, basil, thyme, rosemary, pepper and garlic in a shallow dish. Wash and pat dry the chicken and add to the marinade, turning to coat well. Cover and refrigerate up to 6 hours.

Remove chicken from marinade and rotate in the Flat Standard Basket for 45 minutes or until chicken is cooked through and browned.

NUTRITIONAL ANALYSIS PER SERVING: 262 Calories, 4.4 g Carbohydrates, 31.5 g Protein, 12.8 g Fat, 84 mg Cholesterol, 177 mg Sodium

CITRUS JALAPENO
CHICKEN BREASTS
SERVES 6

6 (6 ounce) chicken breasts, skin removed
1/2 cup thawed orange juice concentrate
1 teaspoon minced lime zest
1/4 cup fresh lime juice
1/4 cup honey
2 teaspoons ground cumin
1/4 teaspoon salt
3 cloves garlic, minced
2 jalapeno peppers, seeded and finely chopped

Wash and pat dry chicken and place in a shallow dish. Whisk together remaining ingredients and pour over chicken, turning to coat. Cover and refrigerate up to 4 hours.

Remove chicken from marinade and rotate in the Flat Standard Basket for 45 minutes or until cooked through and browned.

NUTRITIONAL ANALYSIS PER SERVING: 187 Calories, 16.6 g Carbohydrates, 26.5 g Protein, 1.6 g Fat, 65 mg Cholesterol, 165 mg Sodium

The LEAN
Rotisserie

ORANGE-MUSTARD
CHICKEN BREASTS
SERVES 6

1/4 cup grainy mustard
1/4 cup Dijon mustard
1/4 cup fresh orange juice
1 teaspoon minced orange zest
1 tablespoon balsamic vinegar
1 tablespoon olive oil
2 tablespoons finely chopped fresh parsley
1/4 teaspoon freshly ground pepper
6 (6 ounce) chicken breast halves, skin removed

Combine mustards with orange juice and zest, balsamic vinegar, olive oil, parsley and pepper. Add the chicken and turn to coat well. Cover and marinate 1 to 4 hours in the refrigerator.

Remove chicken from marinade and rotate in the Flat Standard Basket for 45 minutes or until the chicken is cooked through and browned.

NUTRITIONAL ANALYSIS PER SERVING: 164 Calories, 2.4 g Carbohydrates, 27 g Protein, 4.6 g Fat, 65 mg Cholesterol, 324 mg Sodium

CAJUN RUBBED CHICKEN BREASTS

SERVES 4

1 tablespoon paprika
1-1/2 teaspoons garlic powder
1 teaspoon dried thyme, finely crumbled
1/4 teaspoon dried oregano, finely crumbled
1/4 teaspoon cayenne pepper
1/4 teaspoon salt
1/4 teaspoon freshly ground pepper
Vegetable cooking spray
4 (6 ounce) chicken breast halves, skin removed
1 (14-1/2 ounce) can Cajun-style stewed tomatoes,
undrained

In a small bowl combine the paprika, garlic powder, thyme, oregano, cayenne, salt and pepper; stir well. Wash and pat dry chicken and spray with vegetable cooking spray. Then coat with spice rub.

Rotate in the Flat Standard Basket for 45 minutes or until chicken is cooked through. While chicken is cooking, pour the stewed tomatoes into the Warming Tray and cover. Serve chicken topped with a spoonful of tomatoes and juices.

NUTRITIONAL ANALYSIS PER SERVING: 160 Calories, 8.8 g Carbohydrates, 27.3 g Protein, 1.8 g Fat, 65 mg Cholesterol, 468 mg Sodium

The**LEAN**
Rotisserie

Spicy Citrus Rubbed Chicken Breasts

Serves 4

4 (6 ounce) chicken breast halves, skin removed
1 tablespoon minced orange zest
1 tablespoon minced lemon zest
2 teaspoons freshly ground pepper
1 teaspoon onion powder
2 teaspoons garlic salt
1/2 teaspoon cayenne pepper
1 teaspoon brown sugar

Wash chicken and pat dry. Combine remaining ingredients and rub on the outside of the chicken breasts. Let stand 30 minutes.

Rotate in the Flat Standard Basket for 45 minutes or until chicken is cooked through and browned.

NUTRITIONAL ANALYSIS PER SERVING: 131 Calories, 2.6 g Carbohydrates, 26.1 g Protein, 1.5 g Fat, 65 mg Cholesterol, 84 mg Sodium

Ruby Cranberry Glazed Chicken Breasts
Serves 6

1 (8 ounce) can jellied cranberry sauce
2 tablespoons fresh lemon juice
Dash Tabasco
1/4 teaspoon curry powder
6 (6 ounce) chicken breast halves, skin removed
1 tablespoon minced parsley or green onions
Salt and pepper to taste

Puree cranberry sauce, lemon juice, Tabasco and curry powder in the blender or food processor. Wash chicken and pat dry. Season the chicken with salt and pepper. Remove 1/4 cup of the cranberry mixture and brush over the outside of the chicken pieces.

Rotate the chicken in the Flat Standard Basket for 45 minutes or until lightly browned and cooked through. Heat the remaining cranberry mixture in a small saucepan over medium low heat until bubbly.

Serve chicken topped with some of the sauce and a sprinkling of parsley or green onions.

NUTRITIONAL ANALYSIS PER SERVING: 129 Calories, .8 g Carbohydrates, 26.7 g Protein, 1.5 g Fat, 66.7 mg Cholesterol, 75 mg Sodium

SKINNY BUFFALO
CHICKEN DRUMMETTES

SERVES 12

MARINADE:
1/2 cup low-sodium chicken broth
1 tablespoon paprika
2 tablespoons fresh lime juice
1 tablespoon low-sodium soy sauce
1 tablespoon honey
1 teaspoon vegetable oil
1/2 teaspoon salt
1/4 teaspoon hot sauce
1/8 teaspoon cayenne pepper
1/8 teaspoon black pepper

BLUE CHEESE DIP:
1/3 cup low-fat mayonnaise
2 tablespoons minced onion
2 tablespoons nonfat buttermilk
1 clove garlic, minced
1 tablespoon vinegar
1 ounce Blue cheese, crumbled
1 tablespoon minced fresh parsley
1/8 teaspoon freshly ground pepper
Dash of hot sauce
24 chicken drummettes (about 2 pounds), skinned

Combine the marinade ingredients in a large bowl. Add the drummettes. Cover and refrigerate 12 hours.

Rotate the chicken in the Flat Standard Basket for 45 minutes. Arrange on a platter and serve with Blue Cheese Dip.

To make the Blue Cheese Dip, combine all ingredients in blender or food processor; process until smooth.

NUTRITIONAL ANALYSIS PER SERVING: 76 Calories, 2.2 g Carbohydrates, 7.3 g Protein, 4.1 g Fat, 25 mg Cholesterol, 191 mg Sodium

The LEAN
Rotisserie

GREEK HERBED CHICKEN KEBOBS
SERVES 6

1-1/2 pounds boneless skinless chicken breasts
2 tablespoons olive oil
3 tablespoons fresh lemon juice
2 tablespoons water
2 tablespoons minced fresh dill, or
1 teaspoon dried dill
1 tablespoon minced fresh oregano, or
1 teaspoon dried oregano
1 zucchini cut into 3/4-inch rounds
1 red bell pepper cut into 1-inch cubes

Cut chicken into 1-inch cubes. Whisk together the olive oil, lemon juice, water, dill and oregano. Pour over the chicken; toss to coat well. Cover and refrigerate up to 4 hours.

Alternately thread the chicken, zucchini and peppers on the kebob skewers. Rotate the kebobs for 25 to 30 minutes or until the chicken and vegetables are cooked through.

NUTRITIONAL ANALYSIS PER SERVING: 181 Calories, 2.9 g Carbohydrates, 27 g Protein, 6.5 g Fat, 66 mg Cholesterol, 81 mg Sodium

APRICOT GLAZED
CHICKEN KEBOBS

SERVES 6

6 (4 ounce) skinless boneless chicken breast halves
1 cup apricot jam
2 tablespoons prepared horseradish
2 tablespoons minced fresh ginger root
2 tablespoons minced orange zest
2 tablespoons brown sugar
1/4 cup fresh orange juice

Trim chicken breasts of all fat, wash and pat dry. Cut chicken into 1-inch cubes and thread on kebob skewers.

In a small bowl stir together the apricot jam, horseradish, ginger, orange zest, sugar and orange juice. Remove 1/2 the sauce and set aside. Brush the kebobs with the remaining sauce and rotate for 20 minutes or until the chicken is cooked through. Serve with remaining sauce for dipping.

NUTRITIONAL ANALYSIS PER SERVING: 312 Calories, 42 g Carbohydrates, 30 g Protein, 6 g Fat, 72 mg Cholesterol, 12 mg Sodium

The LEAN
Rotisserie

CHICKEN AND MELON SKEWERS
SERVES 6

2/3 cup fresh lemon juice
1/4 cup minced fresh mint
2 tablespoons olive oil
2 tablespoons honey
6 (4 ounce) skinless boneless chicken breast halves
1 small cantaloupe

Combine lemon juice, mint, oil, and honey in a small bowl; stir well and divide in half. Reserve the remaining marinade in the refrigerator.

Cut chicken crosswise into 1-1/2 inch cubes. Peel and seed the cantaloupe and then cut into 2-inch cubes. Add chicken and melon to half the marinade. Cover and refrigerate at least 8 hours, stirring occasionally.

Remove chicken and melon from marinade and alternately thread on the kebob skewers. Rotate for 25 to 30 minutes or until the chicken is cooked through, basting with the reserved marinade for the last 5 minutes.

NUTRITIONAL ANALYSIS PER SERVING: 208 Calories, 114 g Carbohydrates, 26.4 g Protein, 6.2 g Fat, 70 mg Cholesterol, 69 mg Sodium

TROPICAL CHICKEN BROCHETTES
SERVES 6

1/3 cup fresh lime juice
1 tablespoon vegetable oil
1 tablespoon honey
6 (4 ounce) skinless boneless chicken breast halves
12 canned, or frozen and thawed, pearl onions
1 red bell pepper, cut into 2-inch pieces
1 papaya, peeled, seeded and cut into 2-inch pieces
1-1/2 cups fresh pineapple chunks

Combine lime juice, oil, and honey in a shallow dish. Cut chicken into 1-1/2 inch cubes and add to marinade. Cover and refrigerate 8 hours, stirring occasionally.

Remove chicken from marinade, reserving marinade. Alternate chicken, onion, pepper, papaya and pineapple on kebob skewers. Rotate for 25 minutes or until chicken is cooked through, basting with reserved marinade toward the end of the time.

NUTRITIONAL ANALYSIS PER SERVING: 222 Calories, 16.4 g Carbohydrates, 26.6 g Protein, 5.7 g Fat, 70 mg Cholesterol, 66 mg Sodium

The LEAN
Rotisserie

ORIENTAL CHICKEN BROCHETTES

SERVES 4

4 (4 ounce) skinless boneless chicken breast halves
1/4 teaspoon salt
1/4 teaspoon pepper
1 medium yellow bell pepper
1 medium red bell pepper
1 (15 ounce) can whole baby corn, cut in half
1/3 cup Hoisin or teriyaki sauce
1/3 cup honey
1 clove garlic, minced
1/2 teaspoon minced fresh ginger root

Trim chicken and cut into 1-inch cubes. Cut bell peppers into 1-inch squares. Alternate chicken, pepper pieces and corn on kebob skewers.

Stir together the Hoisin or teriyaki sauce, the honey, garlic and ginger. Brush on kebobs and rotate for 25 minutes or until the chicken is cooked through.

NUTRITIONAL ANALYSIS PER SERVING: 284 Calories, 37.3 g Carbohydrates, 24.4 g Protein, 4.5 g Fat, 54 mg Cholesterol, 210 mg Sodium

TANDOORI CHICKEN TIKAS
SERVES 4

2/3 cup plain low-fat yogurt
3 tablespoons paprika
2 tablespoons curry powder
2 teaspoons fresh ground pepper
1 teaspoon vinegar
3/4 teaspoon minced fresh ginger root
1/4 teaspoon salt
2 cloves garlic, minced
4 (4 ounce) skinless boneless chicken breast halves

Combine the yogurt, paprika, curry powder, pepper, vinegar, ginger, salt and garlic in a medium bowl. Trim chicken and cut into 1-inch cubes. Add to the yogurt mixture, turning to coat well. Cover and refrigerate for 24 hours.

Remove chicken from marinade and thread on kebob skewers. Rotate for 25 minutes or until the chicken is cooked through.

NUTRITIONAL ANALYSIS PER SERVING: 181 Calories, 8.9 g Carbohydrates, 29.9 g Protein, 3.1 g Fat, 66 mg Cholesterol, 243 mg Sodium

The **LEAN**
Rotisserie

Light & Crusty Chicken Dijon

Serves 4

4 (4 ounce) skinless boneless chicken breast halves
1/3 cup fine dry bread crumbs
1 tablespoon freshly grated Parmesan cheese
1/2 teaspoon dried thyme
1/4 teaspoon freshly ground pepper
2 tablespoons creamy mustard-mayonnaise blend

Wash and pat dry chicken breasts. Trim chicken and pound to an even thickness of 1/2 inch.

Toss the bread crumbs, Parmesan, thyme and pepper together in a shallow dish. Brush mustard blend evenly over both sides of the chicken. Dredge chicken, coating well, in the bread crumbs. Rotate in the Flat Standard Basket for 20 minutes or until chicken is cooked through.

NUTRITIONAL ANALYSIS PER SERVING: 206 Calories, 7.9 g Carbohydrates, 27.7 g Protein, 6.3 g Fat, 74 mg Cholesterol, 255 mg Sodium

SESAME CHICKEN SUPREMES

SERVES 6

1/4 cup low-sodium soy sauce
1 tablespoon dry sherry
1 teaspoon Oriental sesame oil
1 teaspoon minced fresh ginger root
2 egg whites
6 (4 ounce) skinless boneless chicken breast halves
2 tablespoons toasted sesame seeds

Whisk together the soy sauce, sherry, sesame oil, ginger and egg whites in a medium bowl. Pound chicken to an even thickness and add to the marinade. Let stand 15 minutes.

Remove chicken from marinade and sprinkle with sesame seeds. Rotate in the Flat Standard Basket for 20 minutes or until the chicken is cooked through.

NUTRITIONAL ANALYSIS PER SERVING: 168 Calories, 1.3 g Carbohydrates, 28.8 g Protein, 4.4 g Fat, 66 mg Cholesterol, 419 mg Sodium

Southwestern Chicken with Zucchini-Corn Relish

Serves 4

Zucchini-Corn Relish:
2 large zucchini, coarsely grated
1 cup frozen corn, thawed
1/2 cup cider or white wine vinegar
2 tablespoons vegetable oil
1 tablespoon sugar
1/2 teaspoon salt
1/4 teaspoon celery seed

Rub:
1 tablespoon paprika
1/8 teaspoon ground cumin
1/8 teaspoon dried oregano
1/8 teaspoon dried thyme
1/4 teaspoon salt
1 clove garlic, minced
1 tablespoon olive oil
1 tablespoon fresh lime juice

4 (4 ounce) boneless skinless chicken breast halves

Combine all Relish ingredients in a medium bowl. Cover and refrigerate 2 hours or longer.

Combine all rub ingredients together in a small bowl to form a paste.

Trim chicken breasts and pound to an even 1/2-inch thickness. Rub paste all over chicken breasts, cover and refrigerate for 1 to 2 hours.

Rotate in the Flat Standard Basket for 20 minutes or until cooked through. Serve chicken with drained Relish.

NUTRITIONAL ANALYSIS PER SERVING: 288 Calories, 16.8 g Carbohydrates, 28.6 g Protein, 12.7 g Fat, 35 mg Cholesterol, 348 mg Sodium

CHICKEN FAJITAS
SERVES 8

1 large red bell pepper
1 large green bell pepper
1 large onion
Vegetable cooking spray
1 recipe Southwestern Chicken Breasts (see page 76)
6 small flour tortillas
6 tablespoons nonfat sour cream or yogurt

Cut peppers and onion in halves or thirds. Rotate the vegetables in the Flat Standard Basket for 20 minutes or until very tender. Remove from basket and coarsely chop.

Prepare the chicken and cut into strips. Heat tortillas in Warming Tray while cooking either the vegetables or chicken. Serve tortillas filled with chicken and vegetables.

NUTRITIONAL ANALYSIS PER SERVING: 185 Calories, 18.5 g Carbohydrates, 16.2 g Protein, 4.6 g Fat, 35 mg Cholesterol, 315 mg Sodium

HOT AND SPICY BBQ CHICKEN
SERVES 8

SAUCE:
1 cup ketchup
1/4 cup brown sugar
1/4 cup fresh lemon juice
1 tablespoon Worcestershire sauce
2 teaspoons water
1/2 teaspoon dry mustard
1/8 teaspoon garlic powder
1/8 teaspoon hot sauce

1 teaspoon paprika
1 teaspoon freshly ground pepper
1/2 teaspoon dry mustard
1/4 teaspoon garlic powder
8 (4 ounce) skinless boneless chicken breast halves

Combine the sauce ingredients in a small saucepan. Bring to a boil and then lower heat and simmer for 5 minutes. Divide sauce in half and set aside.

Combine paprika, pepper, dry mustard, and garlic powder. Wash and pat dry chicken and pound to an even thickness of 1/2 inch. Sprinkle with the spices. Rotate in the Flat Standard Basket for 20 minutes, basting with half the BBQ sauce after 15 minutes. Serve with remaining BBQ sauce.

NUTRITIONAL ANALYSIS PER SERVING: 194 Calories, 10.5 g Carbohydrates, 26.3 g Protein, 4 g Fat, 72 mg Cholesterol, 94 mg Sodium

The LEAN
Rotisserie

PINEAPPLE GLAZED SUPREMES
SERVES 4

1 (8 ounce) can unsweetened pineapple slices, undrained
1/2 cup apple juice
1 tablespoon honey
1 teaspoon chicken-flavored bouillon granules
2 tablespoons dried cranberries
4 (4 ounce) skinless, boneless chicken breast halves

To make the Glaze, drain pineapple and set slices aside. Stir together the pineapple juice, apple juice, honey and bouillon in a small saucepan. Bring to a boil over medium heat. Add the dried cranberries. Reduce heat and simmer, covered, for 5 minutes.

Trim chicken and pound to an even thickness between two sheets of plastic wrap. Place in the Flat Standard Basket and top each with a slice of pineapple. Brush with some of the glaze.

Rotate the chicken and pineapple for 20 minutes or until cooked through. Pour the remaining glaze over the chicken and pineapple and serve.

NUTRITIONAL ANALYSIS PER SERVING: 221 Calories, 20.7 g Carbohydrates, 26 g Protein, 3.6 g Fat 70 mg Cholesterol, 275 mg Sodium

SWEET AND TANGY CHICKEN CUTLETS

SERVES 4

1/4 cup dry white wine
1 tablespoon fresh lemon juice
1 tablespoon orange marmalade
4 (4 ounce) skinless boneless chicken breast halves
2 teaspoons poultry seasoning
1/2 teaspoon salt
1/2 teaspoon ground cumin
1/2 teaspoon ground coriander
1/4 teaspoon ground allspice
1/4 teaspoon cayenne pepper
1/4 teaspoon freshly ground pepper

In a small saucepan combine the wine, lemon juice and marmalade. Bring to a simmer, stirring constantly. Cool to room temperature.

Lightly pound the chicken breasts to an even thickness. Add the wine mixture and turn to coat. Cover and refrigerate for 30 minutes or up to 4 hours.

In a shallow bowl stir together the spices. Remove chicken from marinade and coat with spices. Rotate in the Flat Standard Basket for 20 minutes or until the chicken is cooked through.

NUTRITIONAL ANALYSIS PER SERVING: 74 Calories, 4.6 g Carbohydrates, 26.4 g Protein, 5.1 g Fat, 66 mg Cholesterol, 445 mg Sodium

CHICKEN BREASTS WITH TANGY YOGURT SAUCE

SERVES 4

TANGY YOGURT SAUCE:
1 cup seeded and chopped fresh tomato
1/2 cup diced, peeled and seeded cucumber
8 ounces nonfat yogurt
1 tablespoon red wine vinegar
1/4 teaspoon garlic power
1/4 teaspoon dried oregano

4 (4 ounce) skinless boneless chicken breast halves
2 tablespoons fresh lemon juice
1/4 teaspoon dried oregano
1/4 teaspoon freshly ground pepper

To make the sauce, combine all the ingredients in a small bowl, stirring well. Cover and refrigerate 2 hours.

Trim the chicken and pound slightly between two sheets of plastic wrap to an even thickness. Sprinkle with lemon juice, oregano and pepper. Rotate in the Flat Standard Basket for 20 minutes or until cooked through. Serve topped with a dollop of Tangy Yogurt Sauce.

NUTRITIONAL ANALYSIS PER SERVING: 174 Calories, 7.7 g Carbohydrates, 30 g Protein, 2.1 g Fat, 67 mg Cholesterol, 125 mg Sodium

ARTICHOKE & GOAT CHEESE STUFFED CHICKEN BREASTS

SERVES 4

1 (14 ounce) can artichoke hearts
1/4 cup crumbled goat cheese
2 tablespoons chopped chives
1/2 teaspoon grated lemon zest
4 (4 ounce) skinless boneless chicken breast halves
1 teaspoon olive oil
Salt and pepper

Rinse and drain artichokes and coarsely chop. Combine artichokes, goat cheese, chives and lemon zest in a medium bowl; stir well.

Cut a horizontal slit through the thickest portion of each chicken breast half to form a pocket. Stuff 1/4 of the artichoke filling into each pocket; secure with a toothpick.

Brush chicken breasts with olive oil and sprinkle with salt and pepper. Rotate in the Flat Standard Basket for 20 minutes or until chicken is cooked through.

NUTRITIONAL ANALYSIS PER SERVING: 197 Calories, 5.8 g Carbohydrates, 30.2 g Protein, 5.8 g Fat, 73 mg Cholesterol, 149 mg Sodium

SPINACH & BLUE CHEESE
STUFFED CHICKEN BREASTS

SERVES 4

1-1/2 teaspoons olive oil
1/4 cup finely chopped onion
4 cloves garlic, minced
1/2 cup frozen chopped spinach, thawed and drained
2 tablespoons crumbled Blue cheese
1 teaspoon Dijon mustard
4 (4 ounce) boneless skinless chicken breast halves
Salt and pepper

Heat 1/2 teaspoon oil in a small nonstick skillet and sauté onion until tender. Add garlic and sauté 1 minute. Add spinach and sauté 3 minutes. Combine spinach mixture, Blue cheese and mustard in a small bowl. Stir well and set aside to cool.

Cut a horizontal slit through the thickest portion of each breast half to form a pocket. Stuff 1/4 of the spinach filling into each pocket; secure with a toothpick.

Brush breasts with olive oil and sprinkle with salt and pepper. Rotate in the Flat Standard Basket for 20 minutes or until chicken is cooked through.

NUTRITIONAL ANALYSIS PER SERVING: 168 Calories, 2.2 g Carbohydrates, 28 g Protein, 4.7 g Fat, 68 mg Cholesterol, 194 mg Sodium

CHILI AND CHEESE STUFFED CHICKEN BREASTS

SERVES 4

1 (4 ounce) can diced green chilies
4 tablespoons grated Cheddar cheese
4 (4 ounce) boneless skinless chicken breast halves
1 egg white whisked with 2 tablespoons water
1/2 cup crushed reduced-fat Cheddar flavored crackers
1/2 teaspoon paprika

Toss together the chilies and Cheddar cheese. Cut a horizontal slit through the thickest portion of each breast half to form a pocket. Stuff 1/4 of the chili filling into each pocket; secure with a toothpick.

Place the egg and water mixture in a shallow dish. Combine the crushed crackers and paprika in another shallow dish. Dip stuffed chicken in egg whites and then coat with crackers. Rotate in the Flat Standard Basket for 20 minutes or until chicken is cooked through.

NUTRITIONAL ANALYSIS PER SERVING: 299 Calories, 23.5 g Carbohydrates, 32.2 g Protein, 7.8 g Fat, 73 mg Cholesterol, 521 mg Sodium

The LEAN Rotisserie

LEMON CHICKEN WITH MUSHROOMS UNDER WRAPS

SERVES 4

1 tablespoon olive oil
1 clove garlic
1/4 teaspoon dried thyme
1 pound mushrooms, thinly sliced
3 tablespoons fresh lemon juice
1/2 teaspoon salt
1/4 teaspoon freshly ground pepper
4 (4 ounce) skinless boneless chicken breast halves
2 (14 x 12 inch) sheets heavy-duty aluminum foil

In a medium skillet heat the oil with garlic and thyme. Add the mushrooms and toss to coat with oil. Sauté mushrooms until tender. Add lemon juice, salt and pepper.

Trim chicken and pound to an even thickness of 1/2 inch. Lay chicken on one sheet of foil. Top with mushroom mixture. Top with the second sheet of foil and fold the edges over three times to seal the foil packet. Rotate in the Flat Standard Basket for 20 minutes or until chicken is cooked through.

NUTRITIONAL ANALYSIS PER SERVING: 191 Calories, 6.3 g Carbohydrates, 28.7 g Protein, 5.7 g Fat, 66 mg Cholesterol, 348 mg Sodium

CHICKEN CACCIATORE
UNDER WRAPS
SERVES 4

4 (4 ounce) skinless boneless chicken breast halves
1 (16 ounce) can diced Italian tomatoes, drained
1 teaspoon dried oregano
1/4 teaspoon salt
1/4 teaspoon pepper
1/2 cup diced green bell pepper
1 cup thinly sliced mushrooms
2 (14 x 12 inch) sheets heavy-duty aluminum foil

Wash and pat dry the chicken breasts. Stir together the tomatoes, oregano, salt and pepper.

Lay the chicken breasts on one sheet of foil. Top with the tomato mixture and sprinkle with the green pepper and mushrooms. Top with the second sheet of foil and fold the edges over three times to seal the foil packet. Rotate in the Flat Standard Basket for 20 minutes or until chicken is cooked through.

NUTRITIONAL ANALYSIS PER SERVING: 94 Calories, 2 g Carbohydrates, 18.3 g Protein, 1.1 mg Fat, 4.5 g Cholesterol, 225 mg Sodium

The LEAN
Rotisserie

Tuscan Chicken Under Wraps
Serves 4

4 (4 ounce) boneless skinless chicken breast halves
4 garlic cloves, minced
1 tablespoon minced fresh rosemary
1/2 teaspoon salt
1 (15 ounce) can white beans, rinsed and drained
1/2 cup sun-dried tomatoes, snipped
1 cup boiling water
1/2 cup chopped red onion
1 tablespoon olive oil
2 tablespoons fresh lemon juice
2 (14 x 12 inch) pieces of heavy-duty aluminum foil

Trim chicken breasts and pound to an even 1/2-inch thickness. Place chicken on one sheet of foil. Combine garlic, rosemary and salt and sprinkle evenly over the chicken.

Place sun-dried tomatoes in a small bowl. Pour in the boiling water and let stand 15 minutes. Drain, reserving 2 tablespoons of the soaking liquid.

Stir together the beans, drained tomatoes and the reserved liquid, red onion, olive oil and lemon juice. Spoon evenly over chicken. Top with the second sheet of foil and fold the edges over three times to seal the foil packet. Rotate in the Flat Standard Basket for 20 minutes or until chicken is cooked through.

NUTRITIONAL ANALYSIS PER SERVING: 136 Calories, 17.8 g Carbohydrates, 13.1 g Protein, 1.6 g Fat, 16 mg Cholesterol, 126 mg Sodium

MARINARA CHICKEN BUNDLES UNDER WRAPS

SERVES 4

4 (4 ounce) boneless skinless chicken breast halves
2 thin slices prosciutto or ham
2 thin slices Provolone cheese
4 fresh sage or basil leaves
1/2 cup prepared Marinara sauce
2 (14 x 12 inch) sheets heavy-duty aluminum foil

Trim chicken breasts and pound to an even 1/2-inch thickness. Lay one half slice of prosciutto and cheese on each breast. Lay a sage or basil leaf on the cheese. Fold chicken in half to form 4 bundles. Lay bundles on one sheet of foil. Spoon the sauce over the chicken.

Top with the second sheet of foil and fold the edges over three times to seal the foil packet. Rotate in the Flat Standard Basket for 20 minutes or until chicken is cooked through.

NUTRITIONAL ANALYSIS PER SERVING: 191 Calories, 3.5 g Carbohydrates, 30.6 g Protein, 5.5 g Fat, 76 mg Cholesterol, 527 mg Sodium

The LEAN
Rotisserie

BBQ CHICKEN UNDER WRAPS
SERVES 4

4 (4 ounce) boneless skinless chicken breast halves
1/2 cup prepared BBQ sauce
1/2 cup frozen corn, thawed
1/4 cup diced green bell pepper
2 tablespoons chopped cilantro or parsley
2 (14 x 12 inch) sheets of heavy-duty aluminum foil

Trim chicken breasts and pound to an even 1/2-inch thickness. Lay chicken on one sheet of foil. Top with BBQ sauce and sprinkle with corn, bell pepper and cilantro. Top with the second sheet of foil and fold the edges over three times to seal the foil packet.

Rotate in the Flat Standard Basket for 20 minutes or until chicken is cooked through.

NUTRITIONAL ANALYSIS PER SERVING: 173.2 Calories, 8.5 g Carbohydrates, 27.7 g Protein, 2.4 g Fat, 66 mg Cholesterol, 337 mg Sodium

CHICKEN

The LEAN
Rotisserie

The LEAN Rotisserie

TURKEY

The LEAN
Rotisserie

LEAN AND FRESH
ORANGE ROASTED TURKEY
SERVES 10 TO 12

4 cloves garlic, minced
2 teaspoons minced orange zest
1/2 teaspoon dried rosemary, crumbled
1 cup fresh orange juice
2 tablespoons olive oil
1 teaspoon salt
1/2 teaspoon freshly ground pepper
6 orange slices
1 12-pound turkey

In the blender or food processor combine and puree the garlic, orange zest, rosemary, orange juice, olive oil, salt and pepper. Wash and thoroughly dry the turkey, inside and out. Loosen the skin from the breast of the turkey. Pour some of the orange sauce under the skin of the turkey and rub the remaining sauce over the outside. Slip the orange slices between the skin and meat of the turkey breast.

Truss the turkey and rotate on the spit rods for 11 to 12 minutes per pound or until the internal temperature reaches 170 degrees on the instant thermometer inserted in the thigh meat. Let the turkey rest for 20 minutes. Carve as usual and serve.

NUTRITIONAL ANALYSIS PER SERVING: 277 Calories, 3 g Carbohydrates, 40.3 g Protein, 10.4 mg Fat, 166.3 g Cholesterol, 343 mg Sodium

The LEAN
Rotisserie

Maple Roasted Turkey

SERVES 12

1 12-pound turkey
1 tablespoon poultry seasoning
1 tablespoon minced orange zest
1/4 teaspoon salt
1/4 teaspoon freshly ground pepper
3/4 cup fresh orange juice
1/4 cup maple syrup

Wash and pat dry turkey, inside and out. Combine the poultry seasoning, orange zest, salt and pepper and rub over the inside and outside of the turkey. Combine the orange juice and maple syrup in the Warming Tray. Brush on the outside of the turkey.

Truss the turkey and rotate on the spit rods for 11 to 12 minutes per pound or until the internal temperature reaches 170 degrees on the instant thermometer inserted in the thigh meat. Baste the turkey often with the maple glaze. Let the turkey rest for 20 minutes. Carve as usual and serve.

NUTRITIONAL ANALYSIS PER SERVING: 387 Calories, 6.4 g Carbohydrates, 66.4 g Protein, 8.8 g Fat, 198 mg Cholesterol, 258 g Sodium

ROAST TURKEY WITH CRANBERRY GRAVY

SERVES 12

1 12-pound turkey
2 tablespoons olive oil
1 tablespoon minced orange zest
1/2 teaspoon freshly ground pepper
1 (12 ounce) bag fresh or frozen cranberries
3/4 cup sugar
1 (16 ounce) jar turkey or chicken gravy

Wash and pat dry the turkey, inside and out. Combine the olive oil, orange zest and pepper and rub over the inside and outside of the turkey.

Truss the turkey and rotate on the spit rods for 11 to 12 minutes per pound or until the internal temperature reaches 170 degrees on the instant thermometer inserted in the thigh meat. Let the turkey rest for 20 minutes. Carve as usual and serve with Cranberry Gravy.

To make gravy, cook cranberries and sugar in a medium saucepan over low heat, stirring frequently until sugar is dissolved and cranberries burst, about 10 minutes. Puree in blender or food processor. Heat gravy in a medium saucepan. Add the cranberry mixture; stir well and heat through. Serve with turkey.

NUTRITIONAL ANALYSIS PER SERVING: 573 Calories, 38 g Carbohydrates, 71.3 g Protein, 14 g Fat, 199 mg Cholesterol, 1279 mg Sodium

The LEAN
Rotisserie

HONEY MUSTARD TURKEY BREAST
SERVES 6

2 tablespoons honey
1 tablespoon Dijon mustard
1/4 cup dry white wine or vermouth
1 4-pound turkey breast

Whisk together the honey, mustard and wine until smooth. Remove the turkey skin; wash and dry the turkey breast. Spread the honey-mustard mixture over the turkey and let stand for 1 hour. Rotate the turkey breast on the spit rods for 10 minutes per pound or until the internal temperature reaches 165 degrees in the center of the breast. Wait 15 minutes before slicing.

NUTRITIONAL ANALYSIS PER SERVING: 270 Calories, 5.9 g Carbohydrates, 44.2 g Protein, 5.8 g Fat, 132 mg Cholesterol, 143 mg Sodium

TURKEY CUTLETS WITH ORANGE MARMALADE GLAZE
SERVES 4

4 uncooked turkey breast slices (1/2-inch thick)
1/3 cup all-fruit orange marmalade
2 tablespoons grainy Dijon mustard
2 tablespoons dry white wine or vermouth
2 (14 x 12 inch) sheets heavy-duty aluminum foil

Lay turkey breasts on one sheet of foil. Stir together the marmalade, mustard and wine and spread over the turkey. Top with the second sheet of foil and fold the edges over three times to seal the foil packet. Rotate in the Flat Standard Basket for 15 to 20 minutes. Open the packet and serve with juices.

NUTRITIONAL ANALYSIS PER SERVING: 141 Calories, 18 g Carbohydrates, 11 g Protein, 2.7 mg Fat, 28.4 g Cholesterol, 34 mg Sodium

TURKEY AND CHEESE GRINDER
SERVES 8

1/3 cup mango chutney
2 tablespoons low-fat mayonnaise
Dash of cayenne pepper
1 1-pound loaf French bread
8 thin slices leftover Honey Mustard Turkey Breast
Red leaf lettuce
2 ounces Havarti or Monterey Jack cheese, thinly sliced
8 bread and butter pickle slices, chopped
1 medium apple, peeled, cored and sliced into rings

Stir together the chutney, mayonnaise and cayenne pepper. Cut the bread in half horizontally and spread the chutney mixture on the bottom half. Layer with turkey, lettuce, cheese, pickles and apple. Top with remaining bread half. Cut into 8 pieces to serve.

NUTRITIONAL ANALYSIS PER SERVING: 221 Calories, 37.3 g Carbohydrates, 9.9 g Protein, 3.4 g Fat, 9 mg Cholesterol, 703 g Sodium

LEMON HERB TURKEY BREAST
SERVES 6

1 3-1/2 pound turkey breast
2 teaspoons minced lemon zest
2 cloves garlic, minced
2/3 cup fresh lemon juice
1/4 cup chopped fresh basil
1/4 cup chopped fresh mint
1/4 cup white wine vinegar
2 tablespoons chopped fresh oregano
1-1/2 tablespoons olive oil
1/4 teaspoon salt

Remove the skin, wash and thoroughly dry the turkey breast. In a medium bowl stir together the lemon zest, garlic, lemon juice basil, mint, vinegar, oregano, olive oil and salt. Add the turkey breast, turning to coat. Cover and refrigerate for up to 4 hours, turning occasionally.

Remove the turkey from the marinade and rotate on the spit rods for 40 minutes or until the internal temperature reaches 165 degrees in the center of the breast. Let the breast rest for 15 minutes before slicing.

NUTRITIONAL ANALYSIS PER SERVING: 284 Calories, 4 g Carbohydrates, 44.5 g Protein, 9.3 g Fat, 132 mg Cholesterol, 232 mg Sodium

SKINNY CAJUN TURKEY BREAST

SERVES 6

1 quart water
2 tablespoons salt
1 4-pound turkey breast

CAJUN RUB:
1 tablespoon paprika
1-1/2 teaspoons garlic powder
1 teaspoon dried thyme
1/2 teaspoon dried oregano
1/2 teaspoon cayenne pepper
1/2 teaspoon freshly ground pepper

Dissolve salt in the water in a large bowl. Submerge the turkey breast in the salt-water. Refrigerate turkey in brine for 4 hours. Soaking the turkey breast in the salt water yields a very tender, juicy bird after roasting.

Lift turkey from brine and remove skin. Rinse for several minutes to remove all traces of salt. Pat the turkey breast dry. Toss together the rub ingredients and spread evenly all over the turkey breast.

Rotate the turkey breast on the spit rods for 10 minutes per pound or until the internal temperature reaches 165 degrees in the center of the breast. Let the breast rest for 15 minutes before slicing.

NUTRITIONAL ANALYSIS PER SERVING: 247 Calories, 1.2 g Carbohydrates, 44.4 g Protein, 6 mg Fat, 132 g Cholesterol, 143 mg Sodium

The LEAN Rotisserie

TURKEY TENDERLOINS WITH ONION-ORANGE SAUCE

SERVES 4

2 tablespoons Dijon mustard, divided use
2-1/2 teaspoons olive oil, divided use
2 teaspoons fresh lemon juice
1 teaspoon minced lemon zest
1/2 teaspoon dried tarragon
2 cloves garlic, minced
1 (1 pound) bag frozen pearl onions, thawed
2 1/2-pound turkey tenderloins
1/2 cup chicken broth
3 tablespoons frozen orange juice concentrate

Combine 4 teaspoons mustard, 2 teaspoons olive oil, lemon juice and zest, and tarragon and garlic in a small bowl. Brush mustard mixture over turkey tenderloins and rotate in the Flat Standard Basket for 45 minutes or until cooked through and browned.

Meanwhile, heat remaining 1/2 teaspoon oil in a medium skillet over medium heat. Add the thawed onions and sauté 4 minutes or until lightly browned. Add chicken broth and simmer until onions are tender. Add orange juice concentrate and remaining 2 teaspoons mustard; stir well. Slice turkey into 1/4-inch slices and serve with sauce.

NUTRITIONAL ANALYSIS PER SERVING: 238 Calories, 16 g Carbohydrates, 27.2 g Protein, 6.8 g Fat, 59 mg Cholesterol, 305 mg Sodium

TURKEY TENDERLOINS WITH APRICOT SAUCE

SERVES 8

1/2 cup diced dried apricots
1 cup fresh orange juice
1/2 cup apricot preserves
2 tablespoons Dijon mustard
1/2 cup white wine vinegar
2 tablespoons vegetable oil
1 tablespoon low-sodium soy sauce
1 teaspoon coarsely ground pepper
4 1/2-pound turkey tenderloins

In a medium saucepan simmer the apricots in orange juice for about 30 minutes. Stir in apricot preserves until dissolved. Let cool to room temperature. Transfer apricot mixture to blender or food processor. Add the vinegar and oil and puree. Stir in soy sauce and pepper. Cover and refrigerate half of the sauce and pour remaining sauce over turkey tenderloins; cover and refrigerate for 6 to 8 hours.

Remove turkey from marinade; discard this marinade. Rotate turkey tenderloins in the Flat Standard Basket for 45 minutes or until cooked through and browned. Heat the reserved sauce and serve over sliced turkey.

NUTRITIONAL ANALYSIS PER SERVING: 278 Calories, 22.4 g Carbohydrates, 13.3 g Protein, 10.9 g Fat, 66 mg Cholesterol, 177 mg Sodium

The LEAN
Rotisserie

TURKEY SCALLOPS WITH MUSTARD BOURBON SAUCE

SERVES 6

2 tablespoons Dijon mustard
1/4 cup fresh orange juice
1 tablespoon Bourbon
1 tablespoon molasses
1/4 teaspoon salt
1/4 teaspoon freshly ground pepper
6 uncooked turkey breast slices (1/2-inch thick)
1/2 cup chicken broth
2 tablespoons skimmed evaporated milk
2 tablespoons finely chopped cilantro or parsley

Whisk together the mustard, orange juice, Bourbon, molasses, salt and pepper in a shallow dish. Add the turkey slices; cover and refrigerate 2 to 4 hours.

Remove the turkey from the marinade. Place the marinade in a small saucepan along with the broth and evaporated milk. Bring the mixture to a boil and then simmer 5 minutes.

Rotate the turkey in the Flat Standard Basket for 15 to 20 minutes or until cooked through. Serve turkey topped with sauce and sprinkled with cilantro or parsley.

NUTRITIONAL ANALYSIS PER SERVING: 125 Calories, 4.9 g Carbohydrates, 23.1 g Protein, 1.8 g Fat, 39 mg Cholesterol, 1557 mg Sodium

SOUTHWESTERN
SPIT ROASTED TURKEY
SERVES 10 TO 12

1/4 cup paprika
1/2 teaspoon ground cumin
1/2 teaspoon dried oregano
1/2 teaspoon dried thyme
1 teaspoon salt
6 cloves garlic, minced
3 tablespoons olive oil
1 12-pound turkey

Combine the paprika, cumin, oregano, thyme, salt, garlic and olive oil in a small bowl to form a paste. Wash and thoroughly dry the turkey, inside and out. Loosen the skin of the turkey over the breast and spread some of the seasoning mixture directly on the meat. Rub the outside of the turkey with the remaining mixture.

Truss the turkey and rotate on the spit rods for 11 to 12 minutes per pound or until the internal temperature reaches 170 degrees on the instant thermometer inserted in the thigh meat. Let the turkey rest for 20 minutes. Carve as usual and serve.

NUTRITIONAL ANALYSIS PER SERVING: 287 Calories, 2.3 g Carbohydrates, 40.6 g Protein, 12 mg Fat, 166.3 g Cholesterol, 112 mg Sodium

THAI TURKEY NUGGETS

SERVES 4

1 pound boneless turkey breast, skin removed
3 tablespoons minced cilantro
2 teaspoons freshly ground pepper
8 cloves garlic, minced
1/3 cup canned tomato sauce
1 tablespoon distilled white vinegar
1 tablespoon brown sugar
1/2 cup raisins

Cut turkey into 1-1/2 inch cubes. Mix cilantro, pepper and 6 cloves of garlic in a medium bowl. Add the turkey and toss to completely coat the turkey. Thread the turkey cubes on the kebob skewers and rotate for 20 minutes or until the turkey is cooked through.

Meanwhile, in a food processor or blender, combine 2 cloves garlic, tomato sauce, vinegar, sugar and raisins until raisins are chopped. Serve turkey nuggets with sauce for dipping.

NUTRITIONAL ANALYSIS PER SERVING: 215 Calories, 22 g Carbohydrates, 28 g Protein, 2 g Fat, 70 mg Cholesterol, 203 mg Sodium

SKEWERED TURKEY WITH RED PEPPERS
SERVES 6

1/2 cup balsamic vinegar
1 tablespoon olive oil
1/3 cup honey
1 teaspoon dried thyme
1/2 teaspoon dried rosemary
1/2 teaspoon salt
1/8 teaspoon freshly ground pepper
1-1/2 pound boneless turkey breast, skin removed
2 onions, cut into 6 wedges each
2 large red bell peppers, cut into 1-1/2 inch squares

Combine the balsamic vinegar, olive oil, honey, thyme, rosemary, salt and pepper in a medium bowl. Cut the turkey into 1-1/2 inch cubes and add to marinade. Cover and refrigerate at least 2 hours and up to 24 hours.

Alternately thread turkey, onions and red peppers on the kebob skewers. Cook for 15 to 20 minutes or until the turkey is cooked through.

NUTRITIONAL ANALYSIS PER SERVING: 188 Calories, 20.2 g Carbohydrates, 19.7 g Protein, 3.6 g Fat, 48 mg Cholesterol, 413 mg Sodium

The LEAN
Rotisserie

TURKEY MUSHROOM BURGERS
SERVES 6

1 egg white
1/4 cup dry white wine or vermouth
1/3 cup soft French bread crumbs
1/4 teaspoon salt
1/8 teaspoon freshly ground pepper
1/4 cup finely chopped shallots
1 pound ground turkey breast
4 ounces mushrooms, finely chopped
6 onion hamburger buns, split in half

In a medium bowl, beat egg white and wine. Stir in crumbs, salt, pepper and shallots; then lightly mix in turkey and mushrooms. Shape into 6 patties, each about 1/2-inch thick.

Rotate in the Flat Standard Basket for 20 minutes or until cooked through. Place the buns in the Warming Tray to heat during the last 5 minutes. Serve turkey burgers in buns with condiments to taste.

NUTRITIONAL ANALYSIS PER SERVING: 234 Calories, 25 g Carbohydrates, 22 g Protein, 4 g Fat, 49 mg Cholesterol, 369 mg Sodium

TURKEY BROCCOLI PATTIES WITH MUSTARD SAUCE

SERVES 6

1 (10 ounce) package frozen chopped broccoli, thawed
1 pound ground turkey breast
1/2 cup soft whole wheat bread crumbs
1 egg, beaten
1/2 teaspoon ground nutmeg
1/4 teaspoon freshly ground pepper
1 (8 ounce) carton plain nonfat yogurt
1 tablespoon Dijon mustard
1/2 teaspoon Worcestershire sauce

Drain thawed broccoli and pat dry. Finely chop and combine with turkey, bread crumbs, egg, nutmeg, and pepper. Shape into 6 patties. Rotate in the Flat Standard Basket for 20 minutes or until cooked through.

To make mustard sauce, stir together the yogurt, mustard and Worcestershire sauce in a small bowl. Cover and refrigerate until serving time. Serve turkey patties topped with 1 tablespoon of the sauce.

NUTRITIONAL ANALYSIS PER SERVING: 154 Calories, 7.1 g Carbohydrates, 21.4 g Protein, 4.2 g Fat, 77 mg Cholesterol, 186 mg Sodium

The LEAN
Rotisserie

Blue Cheese Stuffed Turkey Burgers

Serves 4

1 pound ground turkey
1 tablespoon white wine Worcestershire sauce
1 egg, beaten
3 tablespoons crumbled Blue cheese
2 tablespoons minced fresh cilantro
4 lettuce leaves
4 whole wheat hamburger buns, split in half

Combine the turkey, Worcestershire sauce and egg. Shape into 8 patties. Combine Blue cheese and cilantro. Place 1 tablespoon cheese mixture in center of 4 patties. Top with remaining patties, sealing edges well.

Rotate in the Flat Standard Basket for 20 minutes or until cooked through. Place the buns in the Warming Tray for the last 5 minutes. Serve burger with lettuce in buns.

NUTRITIONAL ANALYSIS PER SERVING: 285 Calories, 13.7 g Carbohydrates, 31.3 g Protein, 10.9 g Fat, 150 mg cholesterol, 419 mg Sodium

GREEK TURKEY BURGERS

SERVES 4

1 pound ground turkey
1 egg white
1/4 cup fresh white bread crumbs
1-1/4 teaspoons lemon pepper
1/2 teaspoon crushed dried rosemary
1/4 teaspoon salt
1/8 teaspoon freshly ground pepper
1 cup nonfat yogurt
1 clove garlic, minced
1 cucumber, peeled, seeded and grated

Mix turkey, egg white, bread crumbs, 1 teaspoon lemon pepper, rosemary, salt and pepper together gently. Form into 4 patties. Rotate in the Flat Standard Basket for 20 minutes or until cooked through. Stir together the yogurt, remaining 1/4 teaspoon lemon pepper, garlic and cucumber. Serve sauce on burgers.

NUTRITIONAL ANALYSIS PER SERVING: 222 Calories, 7.8 g Carbohydrates, 24.7 g Protein, 9.7 g Fat, 91 mg Cholesterol, 411 mg Sodium

The LEAN Rotisserie

MEDITERRANEAN TURKEY PITAS

SERVES 4

1 pound ground turkey
1 egg white
2 tablespoons plain nonfat yogurt
1/4 cup fresh white bread crumbs
1 clove garlic, minced
1/4 cup minced red bell pepper
1/4 teaspoon ground coriander
1/4 teaspoon ground cumin
1/8 teaspoon cayenne pepper
2 pita breads
1 cup shredded lettuce

Mix turkey, egg white, yogurt, bread crumbs, garlic, red pepper, coriander, cumin and cayenne pepper together gently. Form 4 patties and cook in the Flat Standard Basket for 20 minutes or until cooked through.

Cut the pita bread in half to form two half circles. Open and fill each half circle with a burger and 1/4 cup of lettuce.

NUTRITIONAL ANALYSIS PER SERVING: 268 Calories, 19 g Carbohydrates, 24.2 g Protein, 9.8 g Fat, 90 mg Cholesterol, 294 mg Sodium

SOUTHWESTERN TURKEY BURGERS

SERVES 4

1 pound ground turkey
1 egg white
1/4 cup fresh white bread crumbs
1 teaspoon chili powder
1/2 teaspoon ground cumin
1/4 teaspoon salt
1/8 teaspoon freshly ground pepper
2 canned whole green chilies

Mix turkey, egg white, bread crumbs, chili powder, cumin, salt and pepper together gently. Form into 4 patties. Top each with half a chili and rotate in the Flat Standard Basket for 20 minutes or until the burger is cooked through.

NUTRITIONAL ANALYSIS PER SERVING: 181 Calories, 1.8 g Carbohydrates, 21 g Protein, 9.5 g Fat, 90 mg Cholesterol, 261 mg Sodium

The LEAN
Rotisserie

The LEAN Rotisserie

PORK

The LEAN
Rotisserie

ORANGE SPICED PORK ROAST
SERVES 8

1 2-1/2 pound lean boneless pork loin
1 (6 ounce) can frozen orange juice concentrate, thawed
1/4 cup water
2 tablespoons dry white wine or vermouth
2 teaspoons minced orange rind
1/2 teaspoon ground allspice

Trim fat from pork loin and place in a shallow baking dish. Combine orange juice, water, wine, orange rind and allspice and pour over the pork. Cover and refrigerate for at least 8 hours, turning occasionally.

Remove pork from marinade and rotate on the spit rods for 1 hour or until the internal temperature reaches 160 degrees on the instant thermometer. Remove roast and let stand 10 minutes; slice into 1/2-inch thick slices.

NUTRITIONAL ANALYSIS PER SERVING: 256 Calories, 8.4 g Carbohydrates, 22.4 g Protein, 14 g Fat, 70 mg Cholesterol, 56 mg Sodium

The LEAN
Rotisserie

APPLE BUTTER PORK ROAST

SERVES 8

1 2-1/2 pound lean pork loin roast
1/2 cup apple butter
1/4 cup honey
2 teaspoons brown mustard
1 tablespoon vegetable oil

Combine apple butter, honey, mustard and oil in a small bowl. Trim pork loin of most fat and spread with apple butter mixture. Rotate roast on spit rods for 1-1/4 hours or until meat reaches internal temperature of 160 degrees on the instant thermometer. Let stand 10 minutes before slicing.

NUTRITIONAL ANALYSIS PER SERVING: 300 Calories, 17.2 g Carbohydrates, 22 g Protein, 15.8 g Fat, 70 mg Cholesterol, 73 mg Sodium

APRICOT GLAZED PORK ROAST

SERVES 6

1 2-1/4 pound pork loin roast
1/2 cup apricot preserves
1 tablespoon Dijon mustard
1 teaspoon dried thyme

Combine preserves, mustard and thyme in a small saucepan. Remove 1 tablespoon and brush on pork. Rotate roast on spit rods for 1-1/4 hours or until meat reaches internal temperature of 160 degrees on the instant thermometer. Bring remaining apricot mixture to a boil. Serve with roast.

NUTRITIONAL ANALYSIS PER SERVING: 330 Calories, 18 g Carbohydrates, 27.3 g Protein, 9.2 g Fat, 83 mg Cholesterol, 109 mg Sodium

MUSTARD CRUSTED PORK ROAST
SERVES 14

1 3-1/2 pound lean boneless pork loin roast
2 cloves garlic, minced
1 teaspoon mustard seeds, crushed
1/2 teaspoon dry mustard
1/4 teaspoon onion powder
1/4 teaspoon dried thyme
1/4 teaspoon freshly ground pepper

Trim excess fat from pork. Combine garlic, mustard seeds, dry mustard, onion powder, thyme and pepper and rub over the entire surface of the roast.

Rotate the pork roast on the spit rods for 1-1/4 hours to 1-1/2 hours or until the internal temperature reaches 160 degrees on the instant thermometer. Remove roast and let stand 10 minutes before slicing.

NUTRITIONAL ANALYSIS PER SERVING: 210 Calories, 0.3 g Carbohydrates, 28.8 g Protein, 9.6 g Fat, 88 mg Cholesterol, 70 mg Sodium

CARAWAY RUB PORK ROAST

SERVES 8

2 tablespoons lemon pepper
1-1/2 tablespoons instant minced onion
1 teaspoon caraway seeds, crushed
1/2 teaspoon garlic powder
1/2 teaspoon sugar
1/4 teaspoon freshly ground white pepper
1/2 teaspoon salt
1 3-1/2 pound pork loin roast

In a small bowl combine everything except the pork. Trim the pork loin of all excess fat and rub the spice mixture all over the outside of the meat.

Rotate on the spit rods for 1-1/4 to 1-1/2 hours or until the internal temperature reaches 160 degrees on the instant thermometer. Let stand 10 minutes before slicing.

NUTRITIONAL ANALYSIS PER SERVING: 316 Calories, 2 g Carbohydrates, 31 g Protein, 19.6 g Fat, 98 mg Cholesterol, 333 mg Sodium

PORK ROAST WITH SPICY SEASONING

SERVES 8

1 2-1/2 pound lean pork loin
Grated rind of 2 oranges
1 teaspoon onion powder
3/4 teaspoon ground cumin
1/2 teaspoon garlic powder
1/2 teaspoon cayenne pepper
1/4 teaspoon ground ginger

Trim fat from pork. Toss together orange rind, onion powder, cumin, garlic powder, cayenne and ginger in a small bowl. Sprinkle spice mixture over the pork and let stand 20 minutes.

Rotate the pork on the spit rods for 1 hour or until the internal temperature reaches 160 degrees on the instant thermometer. Remove roast and let stand 10 minutes; slice into 1/2-inch thick slices.

NUTRITIONAL ANALYSIS PER SERVING: 222 Calories, 0.9 g Carbohydrates, 22 g Protein, 14 g Fat, 70 mg Cholesterol, 56 mg Sodium

TEX-MEX PORK TENDERLOIN

SERVES 6

3 tablespoons paprika
1 tablespoon chili powder
1 tablespoon freshly ground pepper
1 tablespoon sugar
1 teaspoon garlic powder
1 teaspoon onion powder
1 tablespoon salt
1/2 teaspoon cayenne pepper
2 pork tenderloins (about 1-3/4 pounds total)

Toss together all the ingredients except the pork until well mixed. Trim all fat and silverskin from the pork tenderloins. Rub the pork all over with the spice mixture to coat well.

Rotate the pork, one skewered on each spit rod, 30 minutes, or until the internal temperature reaches 155 to 160 degrees on the instant thermometer. Let stand 5 minutes and then slice diagonally to serve.

NUTRITIONAL ANALYSIS PER SERVING: 148 Calories, 4.7 g Carbohydrates, 22.6 g Protein, 4.2 g Fat, 67.8 mg Cholesterol, 454 g Sodium

JAMAICAN JERK PORK TENDERLOIN
SERVES 6

1 tablespoon paprika
1/8 teaspoon freshly grated nutmeg
1/2 teaspoon ground cinnamon
6 green onions, white part only
6 jalapeno chilies, halved, with or without seeds
3 tablespoons red wine vinegar
1 tablespoon low-sodium soy sauce
1 tablespoon vegetable oil
1/2 teaspoon salt
1/2 teaspoon freshly ground pepper
2 pork tenderloins (about 1-3/4 pounds total)

In a food processor combine the paprika, nutmeg, cinnamon, green onions, chilies, vinegar, soy sauce, oil, salt and pepper and puree. Pour into a jar and refrigerate overnight to develop flavors.

Trim pork of all fat and silverskin. Spread rub all over the pork, cover and refrigerate for 3 hours. Rotate one tenderloin on each spit rod for 30 minutes or until pork reaches an internal temperature of 155 to 160 degrees on the instant thermometer.

NUTRITIONAL ANALYSIS PER SERVING: 257 Calories, 18.8 g Carbohydrates, 31.6 g Protein, 7.5 g Fat, 86 mg Cholesterol, 352 mg Sodium

The LEAN
Rotisserie

CUMIN-SCENTED PORK TENDERLOIN

SERVES 6

1/4 cup fresh lime juice
2 tablespoons dry white wine or vermouth
1 small jalapeno chili, seeded and minced
1 tablespoon minced fresh cilantro
1 teaspoon freshly ground pepper
3/4 teaspoon garlic powder
1/4 teaspoon ground cumin
2 pork tenderloins (about 1-3/4 pounds total)
Lime wedges for garnish

Combine lime juice, wine, jalapeno, cilantro, pepper, garlic powder, and cumin in a shallow dish. Trim pork of fat and silverskin and add to marinade, turning to coat. Cover and refrigerate 8 hours, turning occasionally.

Rotate the pork, one on each spit rod, 30 minutes or until the internal temperature reaches 155 to 160 degrees on the instant thermometer. Let stand 5 minutes, then slice and serve with lime wedges.

NUTRITIONAL ANALYSIS PER SERVING: 157 Calories, 1.8 g Carbohydrates, 26 g Protein, 4.5 g Fat, 83 mg Cholesterol, 61 g Sodium

GARLIC AND ROSEMARY PORK TENDERLOIN

SERVES 6

4 cloves garlic, minced
1 tablespoon fresh rosemary, minced
3 tablespoons dry white wine or vermouth
2 pork tenderloins (about 1-3/4 pounds total)

With a mini-food processor or mortar and pestle mash the garlic, rosemary and wine into a paste. Trim all fat and silverskin from the pork tenderloins. Rub the pork all over with the garlic paste.

Rotate the pork, one skewered on each spit rod, 30 minutes, or until the internal temperature reaches 155 to 160 degrees on the instant thermometer. Let stand 5 minutes and then slice diagonally to serve.

NUTRITIONAL ANALYSIS PER SERVING: 135 Calories, 1 g Carbohydrates, 22 g Protein, 3.7 mg Fat, 67.8 g Cholesterol, 53 g Sodium

The LEAN
Rotisserie

Italian Seasoned Pork Tenderloin

Serves 6

2 pork tenderloins (about 1-3/4 pounds total)
1 (7 ounce) package dry Italian salad dressing mix
1 tablespoon brown sugar

Trim fat and silverskin from pork. Toss together the salad dressing mix and sugar and rub all over the pork.

Rotate the pork, one on each spit rod, 30 minutes or until the internal temperature reaches 155 to 160 degrees on the instant thermometer. Let stand 5 minutes before slicing across into 1/2-inch thick pieces.

NUTRITIONAL ANALYSIS PER SERVING: 165 Calories, 1.5 g Carbohydrates, 27.8 g Protein, 4.5 g Fat, 86 mg Cholesterol, 1133 mg Sodium

HONEY BOURBON
PORK TENDERLOIN
SERVES 6

2 lean pork tenderloins (about 1-3/4 pounds total)
1/3 cup diced onion
1/3 cup fresh lemon juice
1/3 cup Bourbon
3 tablespoons honey
3 tablespoons low-sodium soy sauce
1 teaspoon minced fresh ginger root
1 tablespoon olive oil
2 cloves garlic, minced
1/4 teaspoon freshly ground pepper
2 tablespoons flour
3/4 cup water

Trim pork of all fat and silverskin. Place in a shallow dish. Whisk together the next 9 ingredients and pour over pork. Cover and refrigerate 1 hour. Remove pork from marinade, reserving 1/3 cup marinade.

Rotate pork, one on each spit rod, for 25 minutes or until the internal temperature reaches 155 to 160 degrees on the instant thermometer.

Place flour in a medium saucepan and whisk in reserved marinade and water. Bring to a boil over medium heat and cook 3 minutes or until thickened, stirring constantly. Slice pork and serve with sauce.

NUTRITIONAL ANALYSIS PER SERVING: 219 Calories, 12.9 g Carbohydrates, 25.4 g Protein, 7.2 g Fat, 79 mg Cholesterol, 403 mg Sodium

The LEAN
Rotisserie

Ginger Teriyaki Pork Tenderloin

Serves 6

1/2 cup low-sodium soy sauce
1/2 cup dry white wine or vermouth
1/4 cup sake or dry sherry
1/4 cup sugar
2 slices fresh ginger root
2 tablespoons water
1 tablespoon cornstarch
2 pork tenderloins (about 1-3/4 pounds total)

To make Teriyaki Sauce, combine the soy sauce, wine, sake or sherry, sugar and ginger in a small saucepan. Bring to a boil and then simmer over medium heat 3 minutes. Whisk water and cornstarch and stir into sauce. Stir over medium heat 1 minute or until thickened. Strain sauce and let cool or refrigerate up to 1 week. Trim all fat and silverskin from pork tenderloins. Place pork in a shallow dish and pour cooled Teriyaki Sauce over them, turning to coat well. Let stand 1 hour or refrigerate up to 8 hours.

Remove pork from marinade and rotate, one skewered on each spit rod, 30 minutes, or until the internal temperature reaches 155 to 160 degrees on the instant thermometer. Let stand 5 minutes and then slice diagonally to serve.

Tip: For a quicker preparation, use 1 cup of a prepared Teriyaki Sauce. You may wish to serve the marinade as a sauce over the sliced pork. If so, transfer the marinade to a saucepan and bring to a boil; then simmer for 3 to 5 minutes before serving.

NUTRITIONAL ANALYSIS PER SERVING: 219 Calories, 16.4 g Carbohydrates, 23.1 g Protein, 3.6 g Fat, 67.8 mg Cholesterol, 764 mg Sodium

ASIAN RUB PORK TENDERLOIN
SERVES 6

2 tablespoons toasted sesame seeds
2 teaspoons ground turmeric
1 teaspoon ground coriander
1/2 teaspoon salt
1/2 teaspoon onion powder
1/4 teaspoon ground cumin
1/8 teaspoon ground cinnamon
2 pork tenderloins (about 1-3/4 pounds total)

In a small bowl stir together all but the pork. Trim fat and silverskin from the pork and rub the sesame mixture over the outside.

Rotate the pork, one on each spit rod, for 30 minutes or until the internal temperature reaches 155 to 160 degrees on the instant thermometer. Let stand 5 minutes before slicing.

NUTRITIONAL ANALYSIS PER SERVING: 181 Calories, 1 g Carbohydrates, 28.7 g Protein, 6.3 g Fat, 86 mg Cholesterol, 246 mg Sodium

LEMON GARLIC PORK TENDERLOIN

SERVES 6

1/2 cup fresh lemon juice
2 tablespoons minced garlic
2 tablespoons minced green onions or chives
1/2 teaspoon minced lemon rind
2 pork tenderloins (about 1-3/4 pounds total)

In a flat dish, stir together the lemon juice, garlic, green onions, and lemon rind. Trim all fat and silverskin from pork tenderloins. Add pork to marinade and turn to coat well. Let stand 1 hour or refrigerate up to 3 hours.

Remove pork from marinade and rotate, one skewered on each spit rod, 30 minutes, or until the internal temperature reaches 155 to 160 degrees on the instant thermometer. Let stand 5 minutes and then slice diagonally to serve.

NUTRITIONAL ANALYSIS PER SERVING: 135 Calories, 2.7 g Carbohydrates, 22.2 g Protein, 3.6 g Fat, 67.8 mg Cholesterol, 53 g Sodium

Asian Citrus
BBQ Pork Tenderloin
Serves 6

1/4 cup fresh orange juice
2 tablespoons fresh lemon juice
2 teaspoons Hoisin sauce
1 teaspoon Asian Hot Sauce or Tabasco
2 teaspoons finely minced fresh ginger root
2 cloves garlic, minced
2 pork tenderloins (about 1-3/4 pounds total)

In a flat dish, stir together the orange juice, lemon juice, Hoisin sauce, hot sauce, minced ginger and garlic. Trim all fat and silverskin from pork tenderloins. Add pork to marinade and turn to coat well. Let stand 1 hour or refrigerate up to 3 hours.

Remove pork from marinade and rotate, one skewered on each spit rod, 30 minutes, or until the internal temperature reaches 155 to 160 degrees on the instant thermometer. Let stand 5 minutes and then slice diagonally to serve.

NUTRITIONAL ANALYSIS PER SERVING: 134 Calories, 1.9 g Carbohydrates, 22.2 g Protein, 3.6 g Fat, 67.8 mg Cholesterol, 154 g Sodium

Orange-Chipotle Pork Soft Tacos

Serves 4

3/4 cup fresh orange juice
1 teaspoon minced orange rind
1/4 cup fresh lime juice
1 canned Chipotle chili in adobo sauce, minced
1 tablespoon vegetable oil
3 cloves garlic, minced
2 tablespoons chopped cilantro
1/2 teaspoon salt
1 pork tenderloin (about 1 pound)
4 corn tortillas
2 cups shredded lettuce

Whisk together the orange juice and rind, lime juice, chipotle, oil, garlic, cilantro, and salt. Trim all fat and silverskin from the pork and cut it lengthwise down the center to within 1/2-inch of the bottom; do not cut all the way through. Open pork and pound gently to flatten. Lay pork in a shallow dish and pour marinade over, turning to coat pork. Cover and refrigerate 4 to 6 hours. Remove pork from marinade, reserving marinade. Rotate in the Flat Standard Basket for 20 minutes or until cooked through. Wrap the corn tortillas in plastic and place in the Warming Tray while roasting the pork.

Transfer reserved marinade to a small saucepan and bring to a boil. Reduce heat and simmer for 3 to 5 minutes. Slice pork into thin strips and serve in tortillas drizzled with sauce and filled with shredded lettuce.

NUTRITIONAL ANALYSIS PER SERVING: 259 Calories, 20.5 g Carbohydrates, 26.4 g Protein, 8.1 g Fat, 74 mg Cholesterol, 369 mg Sodium

BBQ PORK SANDWICHES

SERVES 8

2 pork tenderloins (1-3/4 pounds total)
1 tablespoon paprika
1 teaspoon chili powder
1 teaspoon sugar
1/2 teaspoon garlic powder
1/4 teaspoon salt
1/4 teaspoon freshly ground pepper
1 cup tomato sauce
2 cups light beer
2 tablespoons brown sugar
2 tablespoons fresh lemon juice
2 tablespoons Worcestershire sauce
8 whole wheat hamburger buns, split in half and toasted

Trim fat and silverskin from pork tenderloin. Toss together the paprika, chili powder, sugar, garlic powder, salt and pepper in a small bowl. Reserve 1 teaspoon seasoning mixture. Rub all over the pork tenderloins. Rotate the pork, one on each spit rod, 30 minutes or until the internal temperature reaches 155 to 160 degrees on the instant thermometer. Let stand 10 minutes.

Meanwhile, combine the tomato sauce, beer, brown sugar, lemon juice, Worcestershire sauce and reserved spice mixture in small saucepan. Bring to a boil and simmer 20 minutes. Slice pork very thin and add to sauce to heat through. Divide pork and sauce evenly among the toasted buns.

NUTRITIONAL ANALYSIS PER SERVING: 311 Calories, 33 g Carbohydrates, 26.7 g Protein, 5.6 g Fat, 65 mg Cholesterol, 521 mg Sodium

The LEAN
Rotisserie

PORK AND PINEAPPLE KEBOBS
SERVES 4

1 (8 ounce) can unsweetened pineapple chunks
1 tablespoon minced fresh ginger root
1 tablespoon cider vinegar
1 (6-1/2 ounce) jar Oriental plum sauce
1 (12 ounce) pork tenderloin
24 1-inch pieces red bell pepper

Drain pineapple and reserve 1/4 cup liquid. Combine liquid, ginger, vinegar and plum sauce in a small saucepan and bring to a boil. Cook 1 minute. Set aside.

Trim fat and silverskin from pork and cut into 24 pieces. Thread pineapple chunks, red bell pepper pieces and pork pieces alternately on kebob skewers.

Rotate 25 to 30 minutes or to desired doneness. Serve with pineapple juice mixture drizzled over the kebobs.

NUTRITIONAL ANALYSIS PER SERVING: 247 Calories, 22.3 g Carbohydrates, 18.6 g Protein, 9.4 g Fat, 62 mg Cholesterol, 45 mg Sodium

THAI PORK SATAY

SERVES 8

2 tablespoons fish sauce
1/4 cup fresh lime juice
1/4 cup water
2 tablespoons Oriental sesame oil
1 stalk lemongrass, chopped
1/4 teaspoon crushed red pepper flakes
2 tablespoons minced roasted peanuts
3 cloves garlic, minced
1/4 cup chopped fresh cilantro
1 tablespoon brown sugar
2 pork tenderloins (about 1-3/4 pounds total)

Combine fish sauce, lime juice, water and sesame oil in a large bowl. Add lemongrass, red pepper flakes, peanuts, garlic, cilantro and brown sugar. Trim pork of all fat and silverskin and cut into 1-inch cubes. Add to marinade, cover and refrigerate for 6 to 8 hours.

Remove pork from marinade and thread on kebob skewers. Rotate 20 minutes or until pork is cooked through and browned.

NUTRITIONAL ANALYSIS PER SERVING: 181 Calories, 3.9 g Carbohydrates, 21.8 g Protein, 8.5 g Fat, 65 mg Cholesterol, 53 mg Sodium

The LEAN
Rotisserie

SESAME MUSTARD PORK CUTLETS
SERVES 4

4 6-ounce boneless pork chops
3 tablespoons Dijon mustard
1/4 cup fine dry bread crumbs
1/4 cup freshly grated Parmesan cheese
2 tablespoons sesame seeds
1 tablespoon minced fresh parsley
1/4 teaspoon garlic powder

Trim fat from chops. Spread mustard on both sides of chops. Combine bread crumbs with cheese, sesame seeds, parsley and garlic powder. Dredge the chops in the breadcrumb mixture.

Rotate in the Flat Standard Basket for 20 minutes or until chops are cooked through.

NUTRITIONAL ANALYSIS PER SERVING: 287 Calories, 6.9 g Carbohydrates, 31.1 g Protein, 13.9 g Fat, 82 mg Cholesterol, 556 mg Sodium

THAI PORK CUTLETS
SERVES 4

4 6-ounce boneless pork chops
1 teaspoon grated lemon peel
4 garlic cloves, minced
1/4 cup minced fresh ginger root
1 tablespoon chili powder
1/2 teaspoon ground coriander
1/2 teaspoon freshly ground pepper
1/2 teaspoon crushed red pepper flakes
3 tablespoons water

Trim fat from pork chops. Place the lemon peel, garlic, ginger, chili powder, coriander, pepper, red pepper flakes and water in the blender; blend until smooth. Spread about 2 teaspoons of the paste on each chop, covering both sides.

Rotate chops in the Flat Standard Basket for 20 minutes or until cooked through.

NUTRITIONAL ANALYSIS PER SERVING: 206 Calories, 3 g Carbohydrates, 30.2 g Protein, 7.6 g Fat, 75 mg Cholesterol, 82 mg Sodium

The LEAN
Rotisserie

The LEAN
Rotisserie

BEEF

The LEAN
Rotisserie

BBQ RUB FLANK STEAK
SERVES 6

1-1/2 pound lean flank steak
1 tablespoon brown sugar
1 tablespoon coarsely ground black pepper
1 tablespoon paprika
1 teaspoon powdered mustard
2 teaspoons garlic powder

Combine all ingredients except steak in a small bowl; mix well. Rub spice mixture all over steak. Rotate in the Flat Standard Basket for 25 minutes or until cooked to desired doneness. Slice steak diagonally across grain into 1/4-inch thick slices to serve.

NUTRITIONAL ANALYSIS PER SERVING: 218 Calories, 3.9 g Carbohydrates, 22.5 g Protein, 12.1 g Fat, 58 mg Cholesterol, 436 mg Sodium

TEQUILA LIME FLANK STEAK
SERVES 6

1-1/2 pound lean flank steak
1/4 cup fresh lime juice
1/4 cup Tequila
1/4 cup minced fresh cilantro
3 cloves garlic, minced
2 teaspoons freshly ground pepper

Combine the last 5 ingredients and pour over steak. Cover and refrigerate for 24 hours, turning occasionally. Rotate in the Flat Standard Basket for 25 minutes or until cooked to desired doneness.

NUTRITIONAL ANALYSIS PER SERVING: 223 Calories, 0.7 g Carbohydrates, 22.3 g Protein, 13.2 g Fat, 61 mg Cholesterol, 73 mg Sodium

TERIYAKI MARINATED
FLANK STEAK

SERVES 6

1-1/2 pound lean flank steak
1 cup unsweetened pineapple juice
1/4 cup dry sherry
1/4 cup low-sodium soy sauce
2 cloves garlic, minced
1 teaspoon dry mustard
1/2 teaspoon ground ginger
1/4 teaspoon curry powder

Trim fat from steak and place in a large shallow dish. Combine pineapple juice, sherry, soy sauce, garlic, mustard, ginger and curry powder. Divide mixture in half. Cover and chill half and pour remaining half over steak. Cover and refrigerate for 24 hours, turning occasionally.

Remove steak from marinade and discard marinade. Rotate steak in the Flat Standard Basket for 25 minutes or until cooked to desired doneness.

Meanwhile, pour reserved marinade in a small saucepan and bring to a boil. Keep warm. Place cooked steak in a clean shallow dish and pour on the marinade. Let stand 5 minutes. Slice steak diagonally across grain into 1/4-inch thick slices and serve with juices.

NUTRITIONAL ANALYSIS PER SERVING: 234 Calories, 4.4 g Carbohydrates, 22.7 g Protein, 13.3 g Fat. 61 mg Cholesterol, 305 mg Sodium

RED WINE
MARINATED FLANK STEAK
SERVES 6

1-1/2 pound lean flank steak
1/3 cup dry red wine
1 tablespoon fresh lemon juice
1 tablespoon Worcestershire sauce
1 tablespoon water
1 teaspoon dried basil
1/2 teaspoon dried oregano
1/2 teaspoon dried thyme
1/4 teaspoon salt
1/4 teaspoon ground allspice
1/4 teaspoon cayenne pepper

Trim fat from steak and place in a large shallow dish. Combine wine, lemon juice, Worcestershire sauce, water, basil, oregano, thyme, salt, allspice and cayenne. Divide mixture in half. Cover and chill half and pour remaining half over steak. Cover and refrigerate for 24 hours, turning occasionally. Remove steak from marinade and discard marinade. Rotate steak in the Flat Standard Basket for 25 minutes or until cooked to desired doneness.

Meanwhile, pour reserved marinade in a small saucepan and bring to a boil. Keep warm. Place cooked steak in a clean shallow dish and pour on the marinade. Let stand 5 minutes. Slice steak diagonally across grain into 1/4-inch thick slices and serve with juices.

NUTRITIONAL ANALYSIS PER SERVING: 217 Calories, 1.3 g Carbohydrates, 22.4 g Protein, 13.2 g Fat, 61 mg Cholesterol, 196 mg Sodium

The LEAN
Rotisserie

Korean Beef Kebobs

Serves 8

2 pounds lean top sirloin steak, 1-inch thick
2 tablespoons toasted sesame seeds
1 tablespoon Oriental sesame oil
1/4 cup red wine vinegar
2 tablespoons low-sodium soy sauce
1 tablespoon vegetable oil
2 tablespoons brown sugar
2 cloves garlic, minced
2 tablespoons chopped green onions
1 teaspoon freshly ground pepper
1/2 teaspoon crushed red pepper flakes

Trim fat from meat and cut into 1-inch cubes. Combine sesame seeds, sesame oil, vinegar, soy sauce, oil and brown sugar in a large bowl. Stir in garlic, green onions, pepper and pepper flakes. Add beef cubes, cover and refrigerate 6 to 8 hours.

Remove beef from marinade and thread on the kebob skewers and rotate 15 minutes or until beef is browned on the outside but still pink inside.

NUTRITIONAL ANALYSIS PER SERVING: 292 Calories, 3.7 g Carbohydrates, 21.6 g Protein, 20.9 g Fat, 72 mg Cholesterol, 180 mg Sodium

SIRLOIN STEAK WITH
MUSHROOM WINE SAUCE
SERVES 4

Vegetable cooking spray
1/4 pound fresh mushrooms, sliced
3 tablespoons chopped green onions
3/4 cup dry red wine
3/4 cup water
2 tablespoons tomato paste
1 teaspoon dried tarragon
1 beef bouillon cube
1-1/2 tablespoons chopped fresh parsley
1 1-pound lean beef top sirloin (3/4-inch thick)

Spray a nonstick skillet with cooking spray and add the mushrooms and green onions. Sauté until tender, about 4 minutes. Add wine, water, tomato paste, tarragon and bouillon cube. Bring to a boil then reduce heat and simmer 10 minutes or until liquid is reduced by half. Stir in parsley; keep warm.

Trim fat from sirloin and rotate in the Flat Standard Basket for 20 to 25 minutes or until it reaches desired doneness. Cut steak into four portions and serve each with 1/4 cup sauce.

NUTRITIONAL ANALYSIS PER SERVING: 215 Calories, 5.1 g Carbohydrates, 28.3 g Protein, 8.6 g Fat, 80 mg Cholesterol, 246 mg Sodium

The LEAN
Rotisserie

SIRLOIN STEAK WITH ROASTED GARLIC SPREAD

SERVES 6

2 heads garlic
1 tablespoon olive oil
1/4 teaspoon dried thyme
1/4 teaspoon freshly ground pepper
1 1-1/2 pound sirloin steak (1-inch thick)

Cut the tops of the garlic off, exposing the cloves. Set each head of garlic on a square of aluminum foil and pour 1 tablespoon oil over each head. Wrap garlic up totally sealing the packets.

Rotate in the Flat Standard Basket or the Deep Basket for 45 minutes or until the garlic is very soft.

Remove garlic pulp from heads and mash with any remaining oil, the thyme and pepper. Spread on both sides of the steak.

Rotate the steak in the Flat Standard Basket for 20 to 25 minutes or until it reaches desired doneness. Let stand 5 minutes and then thinly slice across the grain to serve.

NUTRITIONAL ANALYSIS PER SERVING: 256 Calories, .4 g Carbohydrates, 20.7 g Protein, 18.5 g Fat, 72 mg Cholesterol, 57 mg Sodium

CROSS RIB ROAST WITH MADEIRA MARINADE
SERVES 6

1 2-pound Cross Rib Roast
1/2 cup Spanish sherry vinegar or red wine vinegar
1 cup Madeira wine
2 tablespoons olive oil
1/4 cup chopped shallots
2 cloves garlic, minced
2 bay leaves
1 tablespoon Herbs de Provence spice mix
1 teaspoon coarsely ground pepper
1/2 teaspoon salt

Trim roast of most fat. Place in a large bowl. Combine the vinegar, wine, oil, shallots, garlic, bay leaves, Herbs de Provence, pepper and salt and pour over the beef. Cover and refrigerate beef for 8 hours, turning occasionally.

Remove beef from marinade and securely tie up to form as compact a roast as possible. Rotate on the spit rods to desired doneness, or until it reaches 125 degrees internally for medium-rare (about 25 minutes); 135 to 140 degrees for medium (about 30 to 35 minutes), or 150 degrees for well-done (about 40 to 45 minutes.)

NUTRITIONAL ANALYSIS PER SERVING: 427 Calories, 5.6 g Carbohydrates, 24.3 g Protein, 28.2 g Fat, 87 mg Cholesterol, 269 mg Sodium

The LEAN
Rotisserie

The LEAN Rotisserie

LAMB

The LEAN
Rotisserie

JALESCO-STYLE BUTTERFLIED LEG OF LAMB

SERVES 12

1 4- to 5-pound boneless leg of lamb
1 cup fresh orange juice
1 tablespoon minced orange rind
1 tablespoon A-1 Sauce
1 red onion, sliced
1/4 teaspoon garlic powder
1/8 teaspoon crushed red pepper flakes
1/8 teaspoon ground cinnamon
1/8 teaspoon ground cloves

Trim all fat and silverskin from the lamb and set in a flat casserole dish. Stir together the orange juice, orange rind, A-1 Sauce, onion, garlic powder, red pepper flakes, cinnamon and cloves. Pour over the lamb, turning to coat well. Cover and refrigerate for 24 hours.

Remove lamb from marinade and rotate in the Flat Standard Basket for 20 to 30 minutes or cooked to an internal temperature of 135 degrees for medium rare. Slice across the grain and serve.

NUTRITIONAL ANALYSIS PER SERVING: 244 Calories, 3.6 g Carbohydrates, 34.7 g Protein, 9.1 g Fat, 111 mg Cholesterol, 132 mg Sodium

SWEET CURRY
BUTTERFLIED LEG OF LAMB
SERVES 12

1 4- to 5-pound boneless leg of lamb
1/2 cup mango chutney
1/4 cup orange marmalade
1 tablespoon Oriental sesame oil
1/2 teaspoon cayenne pepper
1/2 teaspoon curry powder
1/4 teaspoon salt

Trim all fat and silverskin from the lamb and set in a flat casserole dish. Stir together the chutney, marmalade, sesame oil, cayenne, curry powder and salt in a small bowl. Spread all over the lamb, turning to coat well. Cook immediately or cover and refrigerate for up to 8 hours.

Rotate lamb in the Flat Standard Basket for 20 to 30 minutes or cooked to an internal temperature of 135 degrees for medium rare. Slice across the grain and serve.

NUTRITIONAL ANALYSIS PER SERVING: 275 Calories, 9.7 g Carbohydrates, 34.6 g Protein, 10.2 g Fat, 111 mg Cholesterol, 188 mg Sodium

ROSEMARY AND GARLIC
BUTTERFLIED LEG OF LAMB

SERVES 12

1 4- to 5-pound boneless leg of lamb
1 cup dry red wine
2 tablespoons low-sodium soy sauce
2 tablespoons minced fresh rosemary
1 tablespoon minced garlic

Trim all fat and silverskin from the lamb and set in a flat casserole dish. Stir together the wine, soy sauce, rosemary and garlic. Pour over the lamb, turning to coat well. Cover and refrigerate for 24 hours.

Remove lamb from marinade and rotate in the Flat Standard Basket for 20 to 30 minutes or cooked to an internal temperature of 135 degrees for medium rare. Slice across the grain and serve.

NUTRITIONAL ANALYSIS PER SERVING: 245 Calories, 0.8 g Carbohydrates, 34.6 g Protein, 9 g Fat, 111 mg Cholesterol, 192 mg Sodium

CRANBERRY ROSEMARY
BUTTERFLIED LEG OF LAMB

SERVES 12

1 4- to 5-pound boneless leg of lamb
2 cloves garlic, peeled
2 shallots, peeled
2 tablespoons chopped fresh rosemary
1 cup cranberry juice cocktail
1/2 cup dry red wine
1 tablespoon olive oil
1/4 teaspoon freshly ground pepper

Trim all fat and silverskin from the lamb and set in a flat casserole dish. Puree the remaining ingredients and pour over lamb. Marinate in the refrigerator for 24 hours.

Rotate lamb in the Flat Standard Basket for 20 to 30 minutes or cooked to an internal temperature of 135 degrees for medium rare. Slice across the grain and serve.

NUTRITIONAL ANALYSIS PER SERVING: 261 Calories, 4 g Carbohydrates, 34.6 g Protein, 10.2 g Fat, 111 mg Cholesterol, 157 mg Sodium

LAMB SHASHLIK
SERVES 6

1-1/2 pound lean boneless lamb
3/4 cup dry red wine
1 tablespoon chopped fresh parsley
1 clove garlic, minced
1 teaspoon Worcestershire sauce
1/2 teaspoon freshly ground pepper
1/4 teaspoon dried thyme
2 medium red bell peppers, cut into 1-inch thick strips
3 small yellow squash, cut into 1-inch thick pieces
1/2 pound large fresh mushrooms

Trim excess fat from lamb and cut into 1-1/2 inch cubes. Place cubes in a medium-size bowl. Combine wine, parsley, garlic, Worcestershire sauce, pepper, and thyme. Pour over lamb; cover and refrigerate for 8 hours, turning occasionally.

Remove lamb from marinade and set aside. Transfer marinade to a small saucepan and bring to a boil. Reduce heat and simmer 5 minutes; set aside.

Curl red pepper strips around squash pieces and arrange alternately with mushrooms and lamb on the kebob skewers. Brush skewers with marinade and rotate for 15 minutes or until lamb is just pink in the center.

NUTRITIONAL ANALYSIS PER SERVING: 204 Calories, 7 g Carbohydrates, 24.8 g Protein, 6.4 g Fat, 74 mg Cholesterol, 88 mg Sodium

LAMB BROCHETTES

SERVES 8

2 cups plain nonfat yogurt
2 tablespoons finely chopped fresh mint
1 clove garlic, minced
1/4 cup fresh orange juice
1/8 teaspoon ground cumin
1/2 teaspoon salt
1/4 teaspoon freshly ground pepper
2 pounds boneless lamb, cut into 2-inch cubes
1/2 medium cucumber, peeled and finely chopped

Combine the yogurt, mint, garlic, orange juice, cumin, salt and pepper. Place the lamb in a large bowl and add 3/4 cup of the yogurt mixture, mixing well so that all the meat is well coated. Cover lamb and remaining sauce and refrigerate for up to 4 hours.

Thread the lamb on the kebob skewers and rotate for 15 minutes or until browned, but still pink inside. Stir cucumber into reserved sauce and serve with lamb.

NUTRITIONAL ANALYSIS PER SERVING: 191 Calories, 75 g Carbohydrates, 26.4 g Protein, 6.2 g Fat, 75 mg Cholesterol, 251 mg Sodium

The LEAN
Rotisserie

The LEAN
Rotisserie

SEAFOOD

The LEAN
Rotisserie

JUMBO SHRIMP WITH ROSEMARY
SERVES 4

1 pound jumbo shrimp, shelled and deveined
2 tablespoons olive oil
1 tablespoon minced rosemary
2 cloves garlic, minced
1/2 teaspoon salt
1/4 teaspoon pepper
4 4-inch sprigs rosemary, soaked in water 10 minutes

Place shrimp in a medium-size bowl. Toss with olive oil, rosemary, garlic, salt and pepper. Cover and refrigerate 1 hour. Lay shrimp and rosemary sprigs in the Flat Standard Basket and rotate 15 minutes or until cooked through.

NUTRITIONAL ANALYSIS PER SERVING: 185 Calories, 2.1 g Carbohydrates, 23.2 g Protein, 8.8 g Fat, 173 mg Cholesterol, 435 mg Sodium

BBQ SHRIMP BROCHETTES

SERVES 4

1 pound large uncooked shrimp, shelled and deveined
1/4 cup fresh orange juice
2 tablespoons A-1 Sauce
Salt and pepper to taste

Toss shrimp, orange juice and A-1 Sauce in a medium-size bowl. Season to taste with salt and pepper.

Skewer the shrimp on the metal skewers and rotate for 15 minutes or until shrimp turn bright orange in color. Remove skewers and slip shrimp off onto plates to serve.

NUTRITIONAL ANALYSIS PER SERVING: 130 Calories, 3 g Carbohydrates, 23.2 g Protein, 2 g Fat, 175 mg Cholesterol, 168 mg Sodium

SHRIMP AND RED PEPPER KEBOBS
SERVES 6

1 (8 ounce) can pineapple chunks, undrained
1/4 cup water
2 tablespoons white wine vinegar
1 tablespoon vegetable oil
2 tablespoons low-sodium soy sauce
1/2 teaspoon curry powder
1 pound large fresh shrimp, peeled and deveined
1 large red bell pepper, cut into 1-inch squares

Drain pineapple, reserving 1/4 cup juice. Combine reserved pineapple juice, water, vinegar, oil, soy sauce and curry powder. Add shrimp and toss to coat. Cover and refrigerate 2 hours.

Remove shrimp from marinade and thread on kebob skewers alternately with pineapple and red pepper. Rotate for 15 minutes or until shrimp is cooked through.

NUTRITIONAL ANALYSIS PER SERVING: 125 Calories, 9.8 g Carbohydrates, 13.2 g Protein, 3.8 g Fat, 93 mg Cholesterol, 293 mg Sodium

The**LEAN**
Rotisserie

Spicy Thai Shrimp Satay
Serves 4

3 tablespoons fish sauce or low-sodium soy sauce
2 tablespoons ketchup
1/4 cup sugar
1/4 cup fresh lime juice
1/4 cup water
1 tablespoon vegetable oil
1 tablespoon Thai red curry paste
16 extra large uncooked shrimp, shelled and deveined

Whisk together the fish sauce, ketchup, sugar, lime juice, water, oil, and red curry paste. Add the shrimp and stir to coat well. Let stand for 15 minutes at room temperature or up to 2 hours in the refrigerator.

Skewer the shrimp on the metal skewers and rotate for 15 minutes or until shrimp turn bright orange in color. Remove skewers and slip shrimp off onto plates to serve.

NUTRITIONAL ANALYSIS PER SERVING: 228 Calories, 21 g Carbohydrates, 24 g Protein, 5.4 g Fat, 172 mg Cholesterol, 707 mg Sodium

THAI CHILI-GLAZED SHRIMP

SERVES 4

1/2 cup sugar
1/4 cup water
1/4 cup white vinegar
1/4 teaspoon salt
1 teaspoon chili paste with garlic (or to taste)
2 tablespoons fresh lime juice
1 tablespoon fish sauce
2 tablespoons chopped cilantro
1 pound large shrimp, shelled and deveined

Combine sugar, water, vinegar and salt in a small saucepan. Bring to a boil, stirring until sugar dissolves. Reduce heat and simmer until syrupy, but do not allow sauce to caramelize, about 15 minutes. Remove from heat and stir in chili paste with garlic. Cool. Stir in lime juice, fish sauce and cilantro.

Thread the shrimp on the kebob skewers. Brush with sauce and rotate for 15 minutes or until shrimp are cooked through. Serve with remaining sauce for dipping.

NUTRITIONAL ANALYSIS PER SERVING: 234 Calories, 29.1 g Carbohydrates, 23.3 g Protein, 2.4 g Fat, 173 mg Cholesterol, 307 mg Sodium

SPICY GARLIC SHRIMP TAPAS

SERVES 8

2 pounds uncooked shrimp, shelled and deveined,
leaving tails attached
1/2 cup dry sherry
1/4 cup fresh lemon juice
1 tablespoon olive oil
2 large cloves garlic, minced
2 teaspoons paprika
1 teaspoon dried red pepper flakes
Lemon wedges for garnish
2 (14 x 12 inch) sheets heavy-duty aluminum foil

In a large bowl combine the shrimp, sherry, lemon, oil, garlic, paprika and red pepper flakes. Cover and refrigerate for at least 1 hour. Transfer the shrimp and marinade to one sheet of foil. Top with the second sheet of foil and fold the edges over three times to seal the foil packet.

Rotate in the Flat Standard Basket for 15 minutes. Open packet and serve garnished with lemon wedges.

NUTRITIONAL ANALYSIS PER SERVING: 72 Calories, 1.8 g Carbohydrates, 11.6 g Protein, 1.8 g Fat, 86 mg Cholesterol, 84 mg Sodium

FIRE AND SPICE SHRIMP

SERVES 4

1 pound large shrimp, shelled and deveined
2 tablespoons cracked black pepper
2 tablespoons freshly grated Parmesan cheese
2 teaspoons dried basil
2 teaspoons dried rosemary
2 teaspoons dried thyme
1/4 teaspoon garlic powder
1/4 teaspoon salt

Rinse and pat dry shrimp. Combine remaining ingredients in a medium-size bowl. Add shrimp and toss to coat well. Thread shrimp on the kebob skewers and rotate for 15 minutes or until shrimp are cooked through.

NUTRITIONAL ANALYSIS PER SERVING: 146 Calories, 4.6 g Carbohydrates, 24.7 g Protein, 2.9 g Fat, 174 mg Cholesterol, 350 mg Sodium

The LEAN
Rotisserie

S<small>PICY</small> B<small>AYOU</small> S<small>HRIMP</small>

S<small>ERVES</small> 4

1 pound large shrimp, shelled and deveined
2 tablespoons paprika
2 teaspoons garlic powder
1-1/2 teaspoons dried thyme
1 teaspoon cayenne pepper
3/4 teaspoon dried oregano
1/2 teaspoon salt
1/2 teaspoon freshly ground pepper

Rinse and pat dry shrimp. Combine remaining ingredients in a medium-size bowl. Add shrimp and toss to coat well. Thread shrimp on the kebob skewers and rotate for 15 minutes or until shrimp are cooked through.

NUTRITIONAL ANALYSIS PER SERVING: 139 Calories, 3.9 g Carbohydrates, 24 g Protein, 2.5 g Fat, 173 mg Cholesterol, 437 mg Sodium

Skinny Garlic Shrimp
Serves 6

1-1/2 pounds uncooked shrimp, shelled and deveined
5 tablespoons tomato paste
1/4 teaspoon dried basil
1/2 cup chopped onion
2 cloves garlic, minced
Salt and pepper to taste
2 (14 x 12 inch) sheets heavy-duty aluminum foil

In a medium-size bowl combine the tomato paste, basil, onion, garlic, and salt and pepper. Stir in the cleaned shrimp.

Place the shrimp mixture in the center of one sheet of foil. Top with the second sheet of foil and fold the edges over three times to seal the foil packet. Rotate in the Flat Standard Basket for 15 minutes. Open packet and serve with rice, if desired.

NUTRITIONAL ANALYSIS PER SERVING: 136 Calories, 4.5 g Carbohydrates, 23.8 g Protein, 2.1 g Fat, 173.4 mg Cholesterol, 315 mg Sodium

The LEAN
Rotisserie

CILANTRO LIME SHRIMP PACKETS
SERVES 4

1 pound large raw shrimp, shelled and deveined
1 tablespoon low-sodium soy sauce
1 tablespoon rice vinegar
1 tablespoon fresh lime juice
1 teaspoon minced lime zest
1 teaspoon Oriental sesame oil
1 teaspoon sugar
1/4 teaspoon ground coriander
3 tablespoons chopped fresh cilantro
1/4 pound snow peas, cut in half diagonally
2 (14 x 12 inch) sheets heavy-duty aluminum foil

Place shrimp in a medium-size bowl. Stir together the soy sauce, vinegar, lime juice and zest, sesame oil, sugar, coriander and cilantro. Pour over shrimp, cover and refrigerate 2 hours.

Remove shrimp from marinade and place on one sheet of foil. Top with snow peas. Drizzle 1/4 cup of the marinade over the shrimp. Top with the second sheet of foil and fold the edges over three times to seal the foil packet. Rotate in the Flat Standard Basket for 15 minutes. Open packet and serve shrimp with juices.

NUTRITIONAL ANALYSIS PER SERVING: 154 Calories, 5.7 g Carbohydrates, 24.5 g Protein, 3.2 g Fat, 173 mg Cholesterol, 359 mg Sodium

SCALLOPS EN PAPILLOTE

SERVES 4

1/4 pound fresh asparagus
1 medium red bell pepper
1 (8 ounce) can baby corn, rinsed and drained
1 pound fresh sea scallops
1 teaspoon fresh lemon juice
1 teaspoon dry white wine or vermouth
1/4 teaspoon dried thyme
1/8 teaspoon salt
1/8 teaspoon freshly ground pepper
2 (14 x 12 inch) sheets heavy-duty aluminum foil

Snap off tough ends of asparagus and cut into 2-inch lengths. Cut bell pepper into thin strips in 2-inch lengths.

Place the asparagus, red bell pepper and baby corn in the center of one sheet of foil. Spoon scallops over vegetables and sprinkle evenly with lemon juice, wine, thyme, salt and pepper. Top with the second sheet of foil and fold the edges over three times to seal the foil packet. Rotate in the Flat Standard Basket for 15 minutes. Open packet and serve with rice, if desired.

NUTRITIONAL ANALYSIS PER SERVING: 134 Calories, 9.1 g Carbohydrates, 19.6 g Protein, 5.7 g Fat, 40 mg Cholesterol, 371 mg Sodium

Margarita Scallops

Serves 4

1/2 cup Tequila
3/4 cup dry white wine or vermouth
1/4 cup fresh lime juice
1 teaspoon minced lime zest
1 tablespoon vegetable oil
1/4 cup chopped fresh cilantro
1 pound large sea scallops

Combine the Tequila, wine, lime juice and lime zest with the oil and cilantro in a medium-size bowl. Add the scallops; cover and refrigerate for 4 to 6 hours. Remove scallops from marinade and rotate in the Flat Standard Basket for 15 minutes or until just cooked through.

NUTRITIONAL ANALYSIS PER SERVING: 229 Calories, 4.1 g Carbohydrates, 19.5 g Protein, 4.4 g Fat, 37 mg Cholesterol, 189 mg Sodium

SHERRIED LOBSTER TAILS
SERVES 4

4 (6 ounce) frozen lobster tails, thawed
1/4 cup dry sherry
1 tablespoon fresh orange juice
1 teaspoon minced orange zest
2 teaspoons vegetable oil
1/4 teaspoon freshly ground pepper

Split lobster tails lengthwise. Cut through upper hard shell and meat, but not through the bottom shell. Lift lobster meat through split shell to rest on outside of shell, leaving meat attached to far end of lobster shell.

Stir together the sherry, orange juice, zest, oil and pepper in a small bowl. Brush on the lobster meat. Rotate in the Flat Standard Basket for 15 to 20 minutes or until lobster is opaque. Brush with remaining sherry mixture.

NUTRITIONAL ANALYSIS PER SERVING: 117 Calories, 2.6 g Carbohydrates, 18.7 g Protein, 3 g Fat, 65 mg Cholesterol, 347 mg Sodium

The**LEAN**
Rotisserie

ORANGE DILL FISH FILLETS
SERVES 4

1 pound firm fish fillets
(like shark, halibut, sea bass or swordfish)
2 tablespoons orange juice concentrate
2 teaspoons fresh lemon juice
1 tablespoon minced fresh parsley
1/4 teaspoon dried dill weed
4 thin orange slices

Cut fish into serving-size pieces. Stir together the orange juice concentrate, lemon juice, parsley and dill weed. Add fish and turn to coat. Let stand 5 minutes.

Rotate fish topped with an orange slice in the Flat Standard Basket for 15 to 20 minutes or until just cooked through. Serve immediately.

NUTRITIONAL ANALYSIS PER SERVING: 131 Calories, 1.5 g Carbohydrates, 23.7 g Protein, 2.6 g Fat, 36.3 mg Cholesterol, 62 mg Sodium

TART AND SKINNY
GRAPEFRUIT FISH FILLETS
SERVES 4

**1 pound firm fish fillets
(like shark, halibut, sea bass or swordfish)
1/2 cup fresh grapefruit juice
1 tablespoon low-sodium soy sauce
1 tablespoon chopped fresh parsley
Salt and pepper to taste**

Cut fish into serving-size pieces. Stir together the grapefruit juice, soy sauce and parsley. Add fish and turn to coat. Season fish to taste with salt and pepper.

Rotate fish in the Flat Standard Basket for 15 to 20 minutes or until just cooked through. Serve immediately.

NUTRITIONAL ANALYSIS PER SERVING: 124 Calories, 3.2 g Carbohydrates, 21.3 g Protein, 2.3 mg Fat, 46.5 g Cholesterol, 228 mg Sodium

The **LEAN**
Rotisserie

TANGY HERB
MARINATED FISH STEAKS
SERVES 6

6 (4 ounce) fish steaks
1-1/2 cups dry white wine or vermouth
1/2 cup fresh lemon juice
1 tablespoon minced lemon zest
1/4 teaspoon hot sauce
2 tablespoons olive oil
3 cloves garlic, minced
3 tablespoons mixed chopped fresh herbs
(such as parsley, mint, cilantro, or basil)
1 teaspoon dried oregano
1 teaspoon chopped rosemary
1/4 teaspoon salt
1/4 teaspoon freshly ground pepper

Lay fish steaks in a shallow dish. In a bowl, combine wine, lemon juice and zest, and hot sauce. Stir in oil, garlic, fresh and dried herbs, salt and pepper. Pour over fish; cover and refrigerate 2 to 4 hours.

Remove fish from marinade and rotate fish in the Flat Standard Basket for 15 to 20 minutes or until flaky.

NUTRITIONAL ANALYSIS PER SERVING: 184 Calories, 3.5 g Carbohydrates, 20.6 g Protein, 5.4 g Fat, 49 mg Cholesterol, 155 mg Sodium

PICKLED JALAPENO FISH FILLETS

SERVES 6

1/4 cup fresh lime juice
2 tablespoons pickled jalapeno pepper juice
1 tablespoon vegetable oil
2 teaspoons honey
6 (4 ounce) firm fish fillets
(like shark, halibut, sea bass or swordfish)
1/4 cup sliced pickled jalapeno peppers
Fresh cilantro sprigs for garnish

Combine the lime juice, jalapeno pepper juice, oil, and honey in a shallow dish. Add the fish fillets, turning to coat.

Rotate the fish in the Flat Standard Basket for 15 to 20 minutes or until cooked through. Serve sprinkled with sliced pickled peppers and cilantro.

NUTRITIONAL ANALYSIS PER SERVING: 220 Calories, 3.3 g Carbohydrates, 21.1 g Protein, 13.2 g Fat, 57 mg Cholesterol, 206 mg Sodium

The **LEAN**
Rotisserie

TOMATO-BASIL FISH FILLETS
SERVES 6

6 (4 ounce) firm fish fillets
(like shark, halibut, sea bass or swordfish)
1/3 cup chopped fresh basil leaves
1 (14-1/2 ounce) can diced tomatoes, undrained
1/4 cup balsamic vinegar
1 tablespoon olive oil
2 cloves garlic, minced
2 tablespoons minced green onions
1/4 teaspoon freshly ground pepper
2 tablespoons chopped Italian parsley

Place fish in a shallow dish. Stir together basil, tomatoes with their juices, vinegar, olive oil, garlic, green onions and pepper and pour over fish. Cover and refrigerate for 2 hours.

Remove fish from marinade, reserving marinade. Rotate in the Flat Standard Basket for 15 minutes or until fish is cooked through.

Meanwhile, pour marinade into a small saucepan and bring to a boil. Reduce heat and simmer for 10 minutes. Serve fish topped with tomato sauce and sprinkle with parsley.

NUTRITIONAL ANALYSIS PER SERVING: 144 Calories, 7.4 g Carbohydrates, 21.6 g Protein, 3.4 g Fat, 49 mg Cholesterol, 176 mg Sodium

BBQ FISH FILLETS
SERVES 4

1 tablespoon vegetable oil
1/2 cup chopped onion
1 clove garlic, minced
2 tablespoons cider vinegar
1/2 cup ketchup
1 teaspoon Dijon mustard
1 teaspoon Worcestershire sauce
1 teaspoon hot pepper sauce
2 tablespoons lemon juice
4 (4 ounce) firm fish fillets
(like shark, halibut, sea bass or swordfish)

In a small skillet heat the oil over medium heat. Add the onion and garlic and sauté for 4 minutes or until softened. Remove from heat and stir in the vinegar, ketchup, mustard, Worcestershire sauce, and hot pepper sauce. Let cool.

Drizzle the lemon juice over the fish fillets in a shallow dish. Add the sauce, turning to coat. Cover and refrigerate for 1 hour. Rotate fish in Flat Standard Basket for 15 minutes or until cooked through.

NUTRITIONAL ANALYSIS PER SERVING: 165 Calories, 10.5 g Carbohydrates, 21 g Protein, 4.5 g Fat, 49 mg Cholesterol, 510 mg Sodium

The LEAN Rotisserie

ITALIAN MARINATED SHARK

SERVES 4

1 pound shark
1/4 cup non-fat Italian Salad Dressing
Salt and pepper to taste
2 tablespoons chopped parsley

Cut shark into serving-size pieces. Pour on the salad dressing and turn to coat well. Season with salt and pepper. Cover and refrigerate for 30 to 60 minutes. Rotate fish in the Flat Standard Basket for 15 to 20 minutes or until just cooked through. Serve sprinkled with parsley.

NUTRITIONAL ANALYSIS PER SERVING: 156 Calories, 1 g Carbohydrates, 22.5 g Protein, 6.5 g Fat, 44.2 mg Cholesterol, 103 mg Sodium

JUMBO CHILI SHRIMP

SERVES 4

1 pound jumbo shrimp, shelled and deveined
2 tablespoons vegetable oil
1 tablespoon chili paste with garlic
1 teaspoon low-sodium soy sauce

Place shrimp in a medium-size bowl and toss with oil, chili paste with garlic and soy sauce. Cover and refrigerate for 1 hour. Rotate in the Flat Standard Basket for 15 minutes or until cooked through.

NUTRITIONAL ANALYSIS PER SERVING: 186 Calories, 1.4 g Carbohydrates, 23.1 g Protein, 9.2 g Fat, 173 mg Cholesterol, 217 mg Sodium

JALAPENO LIME SHARK
SERVES 4

1 pound shark
1/4 cup thawed orange juice concentrate
1/2 teaspoon minced lime zest
2 tablespoons fresh lime juice
2 tablespoons honey
1 teaspoon ground cumin
1/4 teaspoon salt
2 cloves garlic, minced
1 jalapeno chili, seeded and finely chopped

Cut shark into serving-size pieces and place in a shallow dish. Whisk together the remaining ingredients and pour over the shark, tossing to coat. Cover and refrigerate 30 minutes. Rotate in the Flat Standard Basket for 15 to 20 minutes or until cooked through.

NUTRITIONAL ANALYSIS PER SERVING: 196 Calories, 12.6 g Carbohydrates, 24.3 g Protein, 5.3 g Fat, 58 mg Cholesterol, 225 mg Sodium

The LEAN
Rotisserie

CREOLE HALIBUT

SERVES 6

3 tablespoons hot sauce
3 tablespoons water
1 tablespoon Creole mustard (or Dijon)
6 (4 ounce) halibut steaks
1/3 cup fine dry bread crumbs
1 teaspoon Cajun/Creole seasoning

Combine hot sauce, water and mustard in a shallow dish. Add halibut steaks, turning to coat. Cover and refrigerate 30 minutes.

Combine bread crumbs and seasoning; toss well. Remove steaks from marinade and dredge in bread crumbs mixture. Rotate in the Flat Standard Basket for 15 to 20 minutes or until cooked through.

NUTRITIONAL ANALYSIS PER SERVING: 151 Calories, 4.3 g Carbohydrates, 24.3 g Protein, 3.1 g Fat, 54 mg Cholesterol, 360 mg Sodium

Halibut with French Mustard Smear

Serves 6

1 tablespoon olive oil
1/2 cup minced shallots
3 cloves garlic, minced
1/4 cup Dijon mustard
1 teaspoon dried rosemary, crushed
4 teaspoons balsamic vinegar
1/4 teaspoon freshly ground pepper
6 (4 ounce) halibut steaks

Heat olive oil in a small nonstick skillet over medium heat. Add shallots and garlic; sauté 3 minutes or until tender. Remove from heat and cool. Stir in mustard, rosemary, balsamic vinegar and pepper. Smear on both sides of the halibut and rotate in the Flat Standard Basket for 15 to 20 minutes or until cooked through.

NUTRITIONAL ANALYSIS PER SERVING: 164 Calories, 3.4 g Carbohydrates, 24.5 g Protein, 5.3 g Fat, 36 mg Cholesterol, 188 mg Sodium

The **LEAN**
Rotisserie

HALIBUT WITH
LEMON HERB MARINADE

SERVES 6

2 teaspoons minced lemon zest
2/3 cup fresh lemon juice
2 cloves garlic, minced
1/4 cup chopped fresh basil
1/4 cup chopped fresh mint
2 tablespoons chopped fresh oregano
1/4 cup white wine vinegar
1-1/2 tablespoons olive oil
1/4 teaspoon salt
6 (4 ounce) halibut steaks

Combine lemon zest and juice, garlic, herbs, vinegar, olive oil and salt in a shallow dish. Add halibut, turning to coat. Cover and refrigerate 30 minutes. Remove fish from marinade and rotate in the Flat Standard Basket for 15 to 20 minutes or until cooked through.

NUTRITIONAL ANALYSIS PER SERVING: 167 Calories, 4 g Carbohydrates, 23.9 g Protein, 6.1 g Fat, 36 mg Cholesterol, 151 mg Sodium

SAFFRON-ORANGE SALMON STEAKS

SERVES 4

4 small salmon steaks
Pinch saffron threads
1 tablespoon very hot water
1/4 cup fresh orange juice
1 teaspoon minced orange zest
1/2 teaspoon Dijon mustard
1/3 cup sweet white wine
1 tablespoon vegetable oil
1 tablespoon minced shallots
1/2 teaspoon coarsely ground pepper
1/4 teaspoon salt
2 tablespoons minced fresh parsley

Place salmon steaks in a shallow dish. Stir saffron into hot water and let stand 5 minutes. Stir saffron and water together with orange juice and zest, mustard, wine, oil, shallots, pepper and salt. Pour over salmon, cover and refrigerate for 1 hour.

Remove salmon from marinade and rotate in the Flat Standard Basket for 15 to 20 minutes or until cooked through. Serve sprinkled with parsley.

NUTRITIONAL ANALYSIS PER SERVING: 251 Calories, 2.6 g Carbohydrates, 34.2 g Protein, 9.4 g Fat, 88 mg Cholesterol, 258 mg Sodium

The LEAN
Rotisserie

SALMON WITH
GINGER MOLASSES MARINADE

SERVES 4

1/2 cup low-sodium soy sauce
1/4 cup molasses
1 tablespoon olive oil
1 teaspoon ground ginger
1-1/4 pound salmon fillet

Whisk together the soy sauce, molasses, olive oil and ginger. Cut salmon into 4 serving-size pieces and place in a shallow dish. Pour on the marinade. Cover and refrigerate for 30 minutes. Rotate in the Flat Standard Basket for 15 to 20 minutes or until salmon is cooked through.

NUTRITIONAL ANALYSIS PER SERVING: 266 Calories, 16.9 g Carbohydrates, 29.8 g Protein, 8.4 g Fat, 74 mg Cholesterol, 1069 mg Sodium

BALSAMIC SALMON WITH MINT
SERVES 4

3 tablespoons balsamic vinegar
1-1/2 tablespoons honey
1 teaspoon vegetable oil
1-1/4 pound salmon fillet
1/2 cup fresh mint leaves, chopped

Stir together the vinegar, honey and oil in a small bowl. Cut the salmon into four pieces and drizzle with the vinegar mixture. Cover and refrigerate 30 minutes. Rotate in the Flat Standard Basket for 15 to 20 minutes or until cooked through. Sprinkle with mint to serve.

NUTRITIONAL ANALYSIS PER SERVING: 202 Calories, 7.4 g Carbohydrates, 28.4 g Protein, 6.1 g Fat, 74 mg Cholesterol, 96 mg Sodium

The LEAN
Rotisserie

Cured Salmon with Tomato-Cucumber Relish

Serves 4

1 pound salmon fillet, skin removed
1/4 cup fresh lime juice
1 green onion, chopped
1 teaspoon sugar
Pinch salt
Dash Tabasco

Tomato-Cucumber Relish:
1 large tomato, seeded and diced
1 small cucumber, peeled, seeded and diced
2 tablespoons seasoned rice vinegar

Cut the salmon into serving-size pieces. Stir together the lime juice, green onion, sugar, salt and Tabasco. Spread on both sides of the salmon. Cover and refrigerate for 4 to 6 hours.

To make the Tomato-Cucumber Relish, toss together the tomatoes, cucumbers and vinegar. Use immediately or set aside at room temperature for up to 2 hours.

Rotate fish in the Flat Standard Basket for 15 to 20 minutes or until just cooked through. Serve immediately topped with Tomato-Cucumber Relish.

NUTRITIONAL ANALYSIS PER SERVING: 225 Calories, 4.3 g Carbohydrates, 23.2 g Protein, 12.5 g Fat, 70 mg Cholesterol, 70 mg Sodium

SALMON WITH
YOGURT DILL SAUCE
SERVES 4

4 small salmon steaks
2 tablespoons fresh lemon juice, divided use
1 medium cucumber
1/2 teaspoon salt
1 teaspoon minced fresh dill or 1/4 teaspoon dried
1 teaspoon minced fresh oregano or 1/4 teaspoon dried
1 clove garlic, minced
Pinch freshly ground pepper
Pinch red pepper flakes
1 cup plain non-fat yogurt

Wash salmon steaks and brush with 1 tablespoon lemon juice. Peel and seed cucumber and then coarsely grate. Toss with salt and let stand for 15 minutes. Drain and squeeze as dry as possible by hand or in several layers of paper towels.

Stir the dill, oregano, garlic, pepper and red pepper flakes into the yogurt along with the remaining tablespoon lemon juice. Stir in the cucumber. Cover and refrigerate for at least 1 hour before serving.

Rotate the salmon in the Flat Standard Basket for 15 to 20 minutes or until just cooked through. Serve topped with the Yogurt Dill Sauce.

NUTRITIONAL ANALYSIS PER SERVING: 373 Calories, 5.5 g Carbohydrates, 38 g Protein, 21.3 g Fat, 112.3 mg Cholesterol, 134 mg Sodium

LEAN AND ZESTY
SWORDFISH STEAKS

SERVES 4

2 (8 ounce) swordfish steaks
2 tablespoons low-sodium soy sauce
2 tablespoons fresh orange juice
1 tablespoon ketchup
1 tablespoon chopped fresh parsley
1 clove garlic, minced
1/2 teaspoon fresh lemon juice
1/4 teaspoon dried oregano, crumbled
1/4 teaspoon freshly ground pepper

Place swordfish in a flat dish. Stir together remaining ingredients and pour over fish turning to coat well. Cover and refrigerate for 1 hour.

Rotate fish in the Flat Standard Basket for 15 to 20 minutes or until just cooked through. Serve immediately.

Tip: Try cutting the swordfish into 1-inch pieces and then rotate on the metal skewers for 15 to 20 minutes. Remove fish from skewers to serve.

NUTRITIONAL ANALYSIS PER SERVING: 151 Calories, 3 g Carbohydrates, 23.1 g Protein, 4.6 g Fat, 44.2 mg Cholesterol, 447 mg Sodium

GRAPEFRUIT AND HAZELNUT SWORDFISH

SERVES 6

1 teaspoon minced grapefruit zest
1/4 cup fresh grapefruit juice
2 tablespoons olive oil
1/4 teaspoon celery salt
1/8 teaspoon freshly ground pepper
2 (12 ounce) swordfish steaks (1-inch thick)
2 tablespoons finely chopped toasted hazelnuts

Combine grapefruit zest and juice with olive oil, salt and pepper in a small bowl. Place swordfish steaks in a shallow dish and pour grapefruit marinade over steaks. Cover and refrigerate for 1 hour.

Remove swordfish from marinade and rotate in the Flat Standard Basket for 15 to 20 minutes or until just cooked through. Meanwhile, pour marinade into a small saucepan and bring to a boil on top of the stove. Simmer for 3 minutes. Serve swordfish sprinkled with hazelnuts and drizzled with boiled marinade.

NUTRITIONAL ANALYSIS PER SERVING: 177 Calories, 1.4 g Carbohydrates, 22.8 g Protein, 8.6 g Fat, 44 mg Cholesterol, 226 mg Sodium

The**LEAN**
Rotisserie

SPICY CRUSTED SWORDFISH WITH CITRUS WALNUT SAUCE

SERVES 4

2 tablespoons Italian seasoned bread crumbs
1/2 teaspoon ground cinnamon
1/2 teaspoon ground ginger
1/2 teaspoon freshly ground pepper
1/4 teaspoon salt
1/4 teaspoon ground cumin
4 (8 ounce) swordfish steaks (about 1-inch thick)
1 teaspoon olive oil
1/2 cup currants or raisins
1 teaspoon minced orange zest
1/2 cup fresh orange juice
2 tablespoons chopped toasted walnuts
1 tablespoon honey

Combine bread crumbs, cinnamon, ginger, pepper, salt, and cumin in a bowl. Rub spice mixture over both sides of the swordfish. Cover and refrigerate 30 minutes. Rotate in the Flat Standard Basket for 15 to 20 minutes or until cooked through.

Meanwhile, heat oil, currants, orange zest and juice, walnuts and honey in a small saucepan. Bring to a simmer. Drizzle sauce over cooked swordfish.

NUTRITIONAL ANALYSIS PER SERVING: 111 Calories, 7 g Carbohydrates, 13.4 g Protein, 3.1 g Fat, 13.4 mg Cholesterol, 125 mg Sodium

---

GINGER LIME SWORDFISH
SERVES 6

2 (12 ounce) swordfish steaks (1-inch thick)
1/4 cup fresh lime juice
1 tablespoon honey
1 teaspoon minced fresh ginger root

Place swordfish in a shallow dish. Combine lime juice, honey and ginger and pour over swordfish. Cover and refrigerate 1 hour.

Remove swordfish from marinade and rotate in the Flat Standard Basket for 15 to 20 minutes or until just cooked through. Meanwhile, pour marinade into a small saucepan and bring to a boil on top of the stove. Simmer for 3 minutes. Serve swordfish drizzled with boiled marinade.

NUTRITIONAL ANALYSIS PER SERVING: 151 Calories, 3.8 g Carbohydrates, 22.5 g Protein, 4.6 g Fat, 44 mg Cholesterol, 102 mg Sodium

The LEAN
Rotisserie

LEMON SAGE SWORDFISH KEBOBS

SERVES 6

3 (12 ounce) swordfish steaks, cut into 1-1/2 inch pieces
1/3 cup fresh lemon juice
1 tablespoon minced fresh sage leaves
1 tablespoon minced garlic
1/4 teaspoon salt
1/4 teaspoon freshly ground pepper
6 large green onions, cut into 2-inch lengths

Place swordfish pieces in a medium-size bowl. Combine the lemon juice, sage leaves, garlic, salt and pepper and pour over fish, tossing to coat well. Cover and refrigerate for 1 hour.

Remove swordfish from marinade and thread on kebob skewers alternately with green onions. Rotate for 15 minutes or until fish is cooked through.

NUTRITIONAL ANALYSIS PER SERVING: 258 Calories, 12.3 g Carbohydrates, 36.5 g Protein, 7.1 g Fat, 66 mg Cholesterol, 266 mg Sodium

LEAN AND TASTY
HAWAIIAN FISH FILLETS
SERVES 4

1 pound firm fish fillets
(like shark, halibut, sea bass or swordfish)
1 tablespoon low-sodium soy sauce
1 tablespoon fresh lemon juice
4 small green bell pepper rings
4 slices fresh tomato
1 (8 ounce) can crushed pineapple, drained
Salt and pepper to taste
2 (14 x 12 inch) sheets heavy-duty aluminum foil

Cut the fish into serving-size pieces. Drizzle fish with soy sauce and lemon juice.

Lay the fish on one sheet of foil. Top with pepper rings, tomato slices and pineapple. Season with salt and pepper. Top with the second sheet of foil and fold the edges over three times to seal the foil packet. Rotate in the Flat Standard Basket for 15 minutes. Open packet and serve with juices.

NUTRITIONAL ANALYSIS PER SERVING: 136 Calories, 5.3 g Carbohydrates, 24 g Protein, 1.7 g Fat, 42 mg Cholesterol, 449 mg Sodium

The LEAN
Rotisserie

HEALTHY SPINACH PARMESAN FISH
SERVES 4

1 pound firm fish fillets
(like shark, halibut, sea bass or swordfish)
1 tablespoon fresh lemon juice
1 (10 ounce) package frozen chopped spinach, thawed
2 tablespoons freshly grated Parmesan cheese
Paprika
Salt and pepper to taste
2 (14 x 12 inch) sheets heavy-duty aluminum foil

Cut the fish into 4 individual servings. Place the fish on one sheet of foil. Drizzle with lemon juice. Squeeze spinach dry and divide evenly into quarters. Spread one part on each piece of fish. Sprinkle with Parmesan, then paprika and finally salt and pepper to taste.

Top with the second sheet of foil and fold the edges over three times to seal the foil packet. Rotate in the Flat Standard Basket for 15 minutes. Open packet and lift fish out onto plates; discard juices.

NUTRITIONAL ANALYSIS PER SERVING: 148 Calories, 2.2 g Carbohydrates, 26 g Protein, 3.5 g Fat, 38.2 mg Cholesterol, 439 mg Sodium

TUNA NICOISE BROCHETTES
SERVES 8

4 (8 ounce) tuna steaks (1-inch thick)
3/4 cup dry sherry
1 tablespoon vegetable oil
1 tablespoon water
1/4 cup low-sodium soy sauce
4 cloves garlic, minced
8 cherry tomatoes
2 large yellow squash, cut into 1/2-inch pieces
1 medium purple onion, cut into 8 wedges
1 (9 ounce) package frozen artichoke hearts, thawed

Cut tuna into 3/4-inch cubes. Place tuna in a large shallow dish. Combine sherry, oil, water, soy sauce and garlic and pour over tuna. Cover and refrigerate for 8 hours.

Alternate tuna, tomatoes, squash, onion and artichoke hearts on kebob skewers. Rotate for 15 minutes or until tuna is barely cooked through.

NUTRITIONAL ANALYSIS PER SERVING: 225 Calories, 8.6 g Carbohydrates, 25.7 g Protein, 7.1 g. Fat, 38 mg Cholesterol, 360 mg Sodium

The LEAN
Rotisserie

TUNA SKEWERS WITH LEMONS AND ONIONS

SERVES 4

1/3 cup chopped fresh oregano
2 tablespoons ground cumin
1 tablespoon crushed red pepper flakes
1/2 teaspoon salt
1/4 teaspoon freshly ground pepper
4 large cloves garlic, minced
1-1/2 pounds tuna steaks, cut into 1-inch pieces
3 small red onions, cut into 8 pieces each
3 lemons, cut into 8 wedges each

Combine oregano, cumin, red pepper flakes, salt, pepper and garlic in a medium-size bowl. Add tuna pieces, tossing to coat. Cover and refrigerate for 30 minutes.

Remove tuna from marinade and alternately thread tuna, onion wedges and lemon on the kebob skewers. Rotate 15 minutes or until the tuna is barely cooked through.

NUTRITIONAL ANALYSIS PER SERVING: 309 Calories, 17.6 g Carbohydrates, 42.4 g Protein, 10.2 g Fat, 65 mg Cholesterol, 375 mg Sodium

TUNA ADOBO

SERVES 4

1/3 cup fresh lime juice
1/2 teaspoon dried oregano
1/2 teaspoon ground cumin
1/4 teaspoon salt
4 cloves garlic, minced
4 (6 ounce) tuna steaks (about 1/2-inch thick)
1 teaspoon olive oil
1/2 teaspoon freshly ground pepper

Combine lime juice, oregano, cumin, salt and garlic in a shallow dish. Add tuna, turning to coat. Cover and refrigerate 1 hour.

Remove tuna from marinade. Brush with oil and sprinkle with pepper. Rotate fish in the Flat Standard Basket for 15 to 20 minutes or until just cooked through.

NUTRITIONAL ANALYSIS PER SERVING: 250 Calories, 1.1 g Carbohydrates, 38.3 g Protein, 9.3 g Fat, 63 mg Cholesterol, 123 mg Sodium

TUNA STEAKS CATALINA

SERVES 6

1/4 cup reduced calorie French salad dressing
2 tablespoons thinly sliced green onions
2 teaspoons minced lemon zest
1/4 teaspoon freshly ground pepper
2 (12 ounce) tuna steaks (1-inch thick)

Combine dressing, green onions, lemon zest and pepper. Place tuna in a shallow dish and pour on the marinade. Cover and refrigerate 1 hour.

Remove tuna from marinade and rotate in the Flat Standard Basket for 15 to 20 minutes or until just cooked through.

NUTRITIONAL ANALYSIS PER SERVING: 178 Calories, 2.7 g Carbohydrates, 26.5 g Protein, 6.2 Fat, 44 mg Cholesterol, 130 mg Sodium

SHERRY GINGER TUNA STEAKS
SERVES 4

4 (6 ounce) tuna steaks
2 tablespoons minced fresh ginger root
2 tablespoons low-sodium soy sauce
2 tablespoons dry sherry
2 tablespoons fresh lime juice
1 tablespoon brown sugar
1 tablespoon vegetable oil
1 tablespoon chopped cilantro
2 tablespoons chopped green onions

Place tuna in a shallow dish. Combine the ginger, soy, sherry, lime juice, sugar, oil, cilantro and green onions and pour over tuna. Cover and refrigerate 2 hours.

Remove tuna from marinade and rotate in the Flat Standard Basket for 15 to 20 minutes.

NUTRITIONAL ANALYSIS PER SERVING: 301 Calories, 4.2 g Carbohydrates, 40.3 g Protein, 11.8 g Fat, 65 mg Cholesterol, 311 mg Sodium

The LEAN
Rotisserie

WHOLE FISH WRAP WITH VEGETABLES
SERVES 4

2 tomatoes, sliced
1/2 red onion, sliced
1 navel orange, peeled and sliced
1 serrano chili, sliced
1 1-1/2 to 2 pound whole lean fish, gutted and scaled
2 tablespoons lemon juice
1/2 teaspoon salt
1/4 teaspoon freshly ground pepper
2 (14 x 12 inch) sheets heavy-duty aluminum foil

Lay tomatoes on one sheet of foil. Top with onions, oranges and chili. Season fish inside and out with lemon juice, salt and pepper. Lay on top of the vegetables. Top with the second sheet of foil and fold the edges over three times to seal the foil packet.

Rotate in the Flat Standard Basket for 15 minutes. Open packet and serve.

NUTRITIONAL ANALYSIS PER SERVING: 176 Calories, 8.7 g Carbohydrates, 31.5 g Protein, 1.4 g Fat, 73 mg Cholesterol, 365 mg Sodium

Salmon Wraps with Orange, Basil and Tomato

SERVES 4

1/4 cup chopped onion
2 cloves garlic, minced
1 teaspoon minced orange zest
1/2 cup dry white wine or vermouth
1/2 cup fresh orange juice
4 plum tomatoes, seeded and chopped
1/2 teaspoon salt
1/4 teaspoon freshly ground pepper
4 (4 ounce) salmon steaks
4 large fresh basil leaves
2 (14 x 2 inch) sheets heavy-duty aluminum foil

Place onion, garlic, zest, wine and orange juice in a small saucepan. Bring to a boil and simmer until reduced to 1/4 cup. Stir in tomatoes, salt and pepper.

Place salmon steaks on one sheet of foil. Top each with a basil leaf and 1/4 of the tomato-orange mixture. Top with the second sheet of foil and fold the edges over three times to seal the foil packet. Rotate in the Flat Standard Basket for 15 minutes. Open packet and serve.

NUTRITIONAL ANALYSIS PER SERVING: 193 Calories, 9.7 g Carbohydrates, 24 g Protein, 4.4 g Fat, 59 mg Cholesterol, 392 mg Sodium

The LEAN
Rotisserie

FISH WRAPS WITH LEEKS
SERVES 4

4 (4 ounce) fish fillets
(like shark, halibut, sea bass or swordfish)
1 tablespoon butter
1/2 cup julienned leeks
2 cloves garlic, minced
1 tablespoon chopped fresh parsley
2 (14 x 12 inch) sheets heavy-duty aluminum foil

Lay fish fillets on one sheet of aluminum foil. Top with bits of butter, leeks, garlic, and parsley. Top with the second sheet of foil and fold the edges over three times to seal the foil packet.

Rotate in the Flat Standard Basket for 15 minutes. Open packet and serve.

NUTRITIONAL ANALYSIS PER SERVING: 124 Calories, 1.3 g Carbohydrates, 20.4 g Protein, 3.6 g Fat, 56 mg Cholesterol, 225 mg Sodium

FISH WRAPS WITH OLIVES AND TOMATOES

SERVES 4

4 (4 ounce) fish fillets
(like shark, halibut, sea bass or swordfish)
1 tablespoon olive oil
2 tablespoons chopped green onions
2 tablespoons chopped black olives
1/2 cup chopped fresh tomato
2 cloves garlic, minced
1/4 teaspoon salt
1 tablespoon chopped fresh parsley
2 (14 x 12 inch) sheets heavy-duty aluminum foil

Lay fish fillets on one sheet of aluminum foil. Drizzle with olive oil and sprinkle with green onions, olives, tomatoes, garlic and salt. Top with the second sheet of foil and fold the edges over three times to seal the foil packet.

Rotate in the Flat Standard Basket for 15 minutes. Open packet, sprinkle with parsley and serve.

NUTRITIONAL ANALYSIS PER SERVING: 135 Calories, 1.9 g Carbohydrates, 20.6 g Protein, 4.7 g Fat, 49 mg Cholesterol, 234 mg Sodium

FISH WRAPS WITH FRESH HERBS

SERVES 4

4 (4 ounce) fish fillets
(like shark, halibut, sea bass or swordfish)
2 teaspoons olive oil
1 teaspoon fresh lemon juice
1 tablespoon chopped fresh dill
1 tablespoon chopped fresh parsley
1/4 teaspoon salt
1/4 teaspoon ground white pepper
2 (14 x 12 inch) sheets heavy-duty aluminum foil

Lay fish fillets on one sheet of aluminum foil. Drizzle with olive oil and lemon juice. Sprinkle with dill, parsley, salt and pepper. Top with the second sheet of foil and fold the edges over three times to seal the foil packet.

Rotate in the Flat Standard Basket for 15 minutes. Open packet and serve.

NUTRITIONAL ANALYSIS PER SERVING: 116 Calories, 0.7 g Carbohydrates, 20.4 g Protein, 3.1 g Fat, 49 mg Cholesterol, 197 mg Sodium

FISH WRAPS WITH
SOY AND PICKLED GINGER
SERVES 4

4 (4 ounce) fish fillets
(like shark, halibut, sea bass or swordfish)
2 teaspoons Oriental sesame oil
2 teaspoons low-sodium soy sauce
2 teaspoons fresh lemon juice
2 tablespoons slivered pickled ginger
1 tablespoon minced fresh chives
2 (14 x 12 inch) sheets heavy-duty aluminum foil

Lay fish fillets on one sheet of aluminum foil. Drizzle with sesame oil, soy sauce and lemon juice. Sprinkle with ginger and chives. Top with the second sheet of foil and fold the edges over three times to seal the foil packet.

Rotate in the Flat Standard Basket for 15 minutes. Open packet and serve.

NUTRITIONAL ANALYSIS PER SERVING: 125 Calories, 2.4 g Carbohydrates, 20.6 g Protein, 3.2 g Fat, 49 mg Cholesterol, 143 mg Sodium

The LEAN
Rotisserie

FISH WRAPS WITH FENNEL, SAFFRON AND ORANGE

SERVES 4

1 tablespoon olive oil
1 tablespoon chopped shallots
1 clove garlic, minced
1/2 cup diced fresh fennel
2 teaspoons minced orange zest
1 tablespoon chopped fresh basil
Pinch of saffron threads
1/4 cup fresh orange juice
4 (4 ounce) fish fillets
2 (14 x 12 inch) sheets heavy-duty aluminum foil

Heat oil in a small skillet and sauté the shallots, garlic and fennel for 2 minutes. Add the orange zest, basil, saffron and orange juice and simmer 2 minutes. Cool slightly.

Lay fish fillets on one sheet of aluminum foil. Spoon on the fennel mixture. Top with the second sheet of foil and fold the edges over three times to seal the foil packet. Rotate in the Flat Standard Basket for 15 minutes. Open packet and serve.

NUTRITIONAL ANALYSIS PER SERVING: 135 Calories, 3 g Carbohydrates, 20.5 g Protein, 4.2 g Fat, 49 mg Cholesterol, 66 mg Sodium

FISH WRAPS WITH LEMON RANCH DRESSING

SERVES 4

4 (4 ounce) fish fillets
2/3 cup fat-free ranch dressing
2 tablespoons fresh lemon juice
1 tablespoon minced chives
2 (14 x 12 inch) sheets heavy-duty aluminum foil

Marinate fish fillets in ranch dressing and lemon juice in refrigerator for 1 hour. Lay fish fillets and sauce on one sheet of aluminum foil. Sprinkle with chives. Top with the second sheet of foil and fold the edges over three times to seal the foil packet.

Rotate in the Flat Standard Basket for 15 minutes. Open packet and serve.

NUTRITIONAL ANALYSIS PER SERVING: 138 Calories, 8.7 g Carbohydrates, 20.3 g Protein, 0.8 g Fat, 49 mg Cholesterol, 461 mg Sodium

The LEAN
Rotisserie

The LEAN
Rotisserie

FRUITS & VEGETABLES

The LEAN
Rotisserie

CUBAN MOJO
VEGETABLE BURRITOS
SERVES 4

1 (4 x 6 inch) piece banana squash, cut into 1-inch cubes
2 zucchini, cut into 1-inch cubes
1 small red bell pepper, cut into 1-inch cubes
2 green onions, sliced
1 serrano chili, minced
2 cloves garlic, minced
3 tablespoons fresh orange juice
3 tablespoons fresh lime juice
1/2 teaspoon ground cumin
1/2 teaspoon salt
4 small flour tortillas
2 (14 x 12 inch) sheets heavy-duty aluminum foil

Lay the squash, zucchini and red bell pepper on one sheet of foil. Sprinkle evenly with the green onions, chili and garlic. Stir together the orange juice, lime juice, cumin and salt. Drizzle over the vegetables.

Top with the second sheet of foil and fold edges over three times to seal the foil packet. Rotate in the Flat Standard Basket for 15 minutes. Place the tortillas in the Warming Tray while the vegetables rotate. Open the foil packet and spoon vegetables on the tortillas, wrap up and serve.

NUTRITIONAL ANALYSIS PER SERVING: 143 Calories, 27.2 g Carbohydrates, 4.2 g Protein, 2.5 g Fat, 0 mg Cholesterol, 156 mg Sodium

213

LEAN & CRISPY
EGGPLANT PARMESAN

SERVES 4

4 3/4-inch thick slices peeled eggplant
1/4 cup fine dry bread crumbs
1/4 cup freshly grated Parmesan cheese
1/2 teaspoon dried parsley flakes
1/4 teaspoon dried oregano
1/4 teaspoon dried basil
1/2 teaspoon paprika
3 egg whites, lightly beaten
1 cup prepared Marinara Sauce

In a shallow bowl or pie plate toss together the bread crumbs, cheese, parsley, oregano, basil and paprika. Dip the eggplant slices in the beaten egg whites and then coat well with the bread crumb mixture.

Place the Marinara Sauce in the Warming Tray on top of the Rotisserie and rotate the eggplant in the Flat Standard Basket for 20 minutes or until tender and crispy. Serve the sauce over the eggplant.

NUTRITIONAL ANALYSIS PER SERVING: 154 Calories, 18.1 g Carbohydrates, 8.2 g Protein, 5.7 g Fat, 5.9 mg Cholesterol, 553 mg Sodium

EGGPLANT WITH
SESAME MARINADE
SERVES 4

1 1-pound eggplant, cut lengthwise in 1-inch slices
1/2 teaspoon salt
1 teaspoon sesame seeds
1/8 teaspoon crushed red pepper flakes
1 tablespoon rice vinegar
2 teaspoons Oriental sesame oil
1/2 teaspoon fresh lemon juice
2 cloves garlic, minced

Place eggplant slices on several layers of paper towels; sprinkle salt over cut sides. Let stand 15 minutes; blot dry with paper towels.

Combine sesame seeds, red pepper flakes, rice vinegar, sesame oil, lemon juice and garlic in a small bowl. Brush over the eggplant slices; let stand 10 minutes. Rotate in the Flat Standard Basket for 20 minutes or until tender.

NUTRITIONAL ANALYSIS PER SERVING: 58 Calories, 8.1 g Carbohydrates, 1.5 g Protein, 2.9 g Fat, 0 mg Cholesterol, 152 mg Sodium

The LEAN Rotisserie

ROASTED EGGPLANT AND GARLIC PUREE SALAD

SERVES 2

1 eggplant (about 1-1/2 pounds)
2 large cloves garlic, thinly sliced
Grated zest and juice of 1 lemon
1 tablespoon olive oil
1 teaspoon minced parsley
1 tablespoon thick non-fat yogurt
Salt and pepper to taste
2 large lettuce leaves
1 tomato, cut into 4 wedges

Cut the eggplant in half lengthwise. With a sharp knife, make small cuts in the cut surface of the eggplant and insert the garlic slices. Rotate the eggplant in the Flat Standard Basket for 40 minutes or until thoroughly soft and wrinkled all over.

Scrape the meat of the eggplant and the garlic out of the skin and puree in the food processor or with a food mill. Stir in the lemon zest and juice, olive oil, parsley and yogurt. Season to taste with salt and pepper. Cover and refrigerate at least 1 hour to cool.

To serve, lay a lettuce leaf on each plate. Top with half of the eggplant in a mound. Lay 2 tomato wedges at the side of the eggplant puree.

NUTRITIONAL ANALYSIS PER SERVING: 142 Calories, 18.8 g Carbohydrates, 3.2 g Protein, 7.7 g Fat, 1.6 mg Cholesterol, 18 mg Sodium

SPAGHETTI SQUASH WITH SALSA FRESCA

SERVES 6

1 4-pound spaghetti squash
1-1/2 cups fresh salsa
2 tablespoons fresh cilantro
3 tablespoons crumbled Feta cheese

Cut the squash in half lengthwise. Rotate in the Flat Standard Basket for 15 to 20 minutes or until soft. Cool slightly. Using a fork, remove spaghetti-like strands, discard shells. Place squash strands in a bowl.

Heat salsa in a small saucepan until bubbly. Stir in cilantro. Serve over squash topped with Feta cheese.

NUTRITIONAL ANALYSIS PER SERVING: 62 Calories, 12.3 g Carbohydrates, 2.3 g Protein, 1 g Fat, 1 mg Cholesterol, 289 mg Sodium

The LEAN
Rotisserie

LIME MARINATED ROASTED PEPPERS
SERVES 10

2 red bell peppers
2 yellow bell pepper
2 green bell peppers
1/3 cup fresh lime juice
1 teaspoon minced lime zest
1/4 cup dry white wine or vermouth
1 can Chipotle chilies in adobo sauce
3 cloves garlic, minced
1/4 cup chopped fresh cilantro

Cut the peppers in halves or thirds and remove all seeds and membrane. Rotate in the Flat Standard Basket in the Pause to Sear mode with the skin side facing the heating element, until skins are blackened, about 15 to 20 minutes. Transfer to a paper bag and let stand 10 minutes. Remove from bag and peel off skins and cut into thick strips.

Puree the lime juice and zest, wine, chili and garlic in the blender or food processor. Stir in the cilantro and pour over the peppers. Cover and refrigerate for at least 6 hours before serving.

NUTRITIONAL ANALYSIS PER SERVING: 31 Calories, 5.7 g Carbohydrates, 0.9 g Protein, .2 g Fat, 0 mg Cholesterol, 5 mg Sodium

KOREAN-STYLE SESAME
PORTOBELLO MUSHROOMS

SERVES 4

4 large Portobello mushrooms
2 green onions, finely chopped
3 cloves garlic, minced
1/2 cup soy sauce
2 tablespoons brown sugar
2 tablespoons dry sherry
1/4 teaspoon freshly ground pepper
1 tablespoon toasted sesame seeds

Trim the stems from the mushrooms and using a spoon, scrape out the dark brown gills on the underside of the mushrooms.

Stir together the green onions, garlic, soy sauce, brown sugar, dry sherry and pepper. Add the mushrooms and turn to coat. Let stand for 30 to 60 minutes.

Remove mushrooms from marinade and place in the Flat Standard Basket. Rotate for 20 minutes or until mushrooms are tender. Sprinkle with sesame seeds.

NUTRITIONAL ANALYSIS PER SERVING: 44 Calories, 4.7 g Carbohydrates, 2 g Protein, 1.4 g Fat, 0 mg Cholesterol, 1065 mg Sodium

The LEAN Rotisserie

PICANTE PORTOBELLOS

SERVES 4

4 large Portobello mushrooms
Vegetable cooking spray
1/2 cup prepared Picante salsa
1 clove garlic, minced
1 tablespoon minced cilantro

Trim the stems from the mushrooms and using a spoon, scrape out the dark brown gills on the underside of the mushrooms. Spray the mushrooms with vegetable cooking spray and rotate in the Flat Standard Basket for 20 minutes or until tender.

In a small saucepan, heat the Picante salsa with the garlic and bring to a boil. Simmer for 2 minutes. Stir in the cilantro and drizzle over mushrooms to serve.

NUTRITIONAL ANALYSIS PER SERVING: 37 Calories, 6.5 g Carbohydrates, 0.9 g Protein, 1.3 g Fat, 0 mg Cholesterol, 26 mg Sodium

PORTOBELLO CLUB SANDWICH

SERVES 4

4 4-inch Portobello mushrooms
2 tablespoons balsamic vinegar
2 tablespoons fresh lemon juice
2 tablespoons water
1 teaspoon olive oil
2 teaspoons dried Italian seasoning
1 teaspoon minced fresh rosemary
1/2 teaspoon freshly ground pepper
2 garlic cloves, minced
1/4 cup non-fat mayonnaise
4 onion or Kaiser rolls, toasted
4 thin slices Provolone cheese
4 lettuce leaves
4 thin slices tomato

Trim the stems from the mushrooms and using a spoon, scrape out the dark brown gills on the underside of the mushrooms. Combine the vinegar, lemon juice, water, olive oil, Italian seasoning, rosemary, pepper and garlic in a bowl. Add the mushrooms and let stand 30 minutes.

Remove the mushrooms from the marinade and rotate in the Flat Standard Basket for 20 minutes or until tender. Spread rolls with mayonnaise and top with mushrooms, cheese, lettuce and tomato.

NUTRITIONAL ANALYSIS PER SERVING: 274 Calories, 38.7 g Carbohydrates, 11.4 g Protein, 9 g Fat, 10 mg Cholesterol, 542 mg Sodium

Roasted Vegetable Salsa

Makes 2 Cups

1 medium red onion, peeled and halved crosswise
1 red bell pepper, quartered and seeded
1 green bell pepper, quartered and seeded
2 jalapeno chilies, halved and seeded
Vegetable cooking spray
2 large tomatoes, seeded and chopped
3 tablespoons tomato juice
1 teaspoon chili powder
1/8 teaspoon ground cumin
1 tablespoon fresh lime juice
1/2 teaspoon garlic salt

Arrange onion, bell peppers and jalapeno in Flat Standard Basket. Spray with cooking spray on both sides. Rotate for 10 to 15 minutes or until vegetables are tender. Remove vegetables and coarsely chop.

Toss chopped vegetables with tomatoes, tomato juice, chili powder, cumin, lime juice and garlic salt. Let stand at room temperature for 30 minutes before serving.

NUTRITIONAL ANALYSIS PER SERVING: 46 Calories, 10.6 g Carbohydrates, 1.7 g Protein, 0.5 g Fat, 9 mg Cholesterol, 58 mg Sodium

ROASTED MIXED VEGETABLES
SERVES 6

1 cup large broccoli florets
1 cup large cauliflower florets
2 carrots, peeled and cut into 2-inch pieces
1/2 pound large button mushrooms, stems trimmed
Vegetable cooking spray
1 teaspoon mixed Italian dried herbs
1/4 teaspoon salt
1/4 teaspoon freshly ground pepper

Combine broccoli, cauliflower, carrots and mushrooms in a large bowl. Spray with vegetable cooking spray, tossing to coat. Toss in the herbs, salt and pepper. Turn vegetables into the Flat Standard Basket and rotate for 20 to 25 minutes or until vegetables are tender.

NUTRITIONAL ANALYSIS PER SERVING: 26 Calories, 5.4 g Carbohydrates, 1.6 g Protein, 0.3 g Fat, 0 mg Cholesterol, 105 mg Sodium

The LEAN Rotisserie

BALSAMIC ROASTED ONIONS

SERVES 6

3 large sweet onions (about 1-3/4 pounds)
1/4 cup balsamic vinegar
1 tablespoon olive oil
1 teaspoon dried thyme
1/2 teaspoon dried basil
1/4 teaspoon salt
1/8 teaspoon freshly ground pepper
2 (14 x 12 inch) sheets heavy-duty aluminum foil

Peel onions, leaving roots intact; cut each into 6 wedges. Combine vinegar, olive oil, thyme, basil, salt and pepper in a large bowl. Add onions and toss gently to coat. Turn onion mixture out onto one sheet of foil. Top with second sheet of foil and fold edges over three times to seal the foil packet.

Rotate in the Flat Standard Basket for 20 minutes. Open packet and serve.

NUTRITIONAL ANALYSIS PER SERVING: 72 Calories, 11.8 g Carbohydrates, 1.6 g Protein, 2.6 g Fat, 0 mg Cholesterol, 102 mg Sodium

DIJON ONION RINGS

SERVES 4

3 tablespoons Dijon mustard
1 tablespoon lemon juice
1-1/2 teaspoons olive oil
1 teaspoon dried thyme
1 teaspoon julienne-cut lemon zest
3 medium onions, sliced 1/4-inch thick
2 (14 x 12 inch) sheets heavy-duty aluminum foil

Combine the mustard, lemon juice, olive oil and thyme in a large bowl. Toss in the lemon zest and onion slices. Turn onion mixture out onto one sheet of foil. Top with second sheet of foil and fold edges over three times to seal the foil packet.

Rotate in the Flat Standard Basket for 20 minutes. Open packet and serve.

NUTRITIONAL ANALYSIS PER SERVING: 59 Calories, 7.5 g Carbohydrates, 0.9 g Protein, 2.7 g Fat, 0 mg Cholesterol, 337 mg Sodium

The LEAN
Rotisserie

CAJUN ROASTED POTATOES
SERVES 6

3 medium red potatoes
1 tablespoon paprika
1 teaspoon garlic powder
1 teaspoon dried thyme
1/4 teaspoon dried oregano
1/4 teaspoon cayenne pepper
1/2 teaspoon salt
1/2 teaspoon freshly ground pepper
Olive oil non-stick spray

Scrub the potatoes and cut in half. Toss together the paprika, garlic powder, thyme, oregano, cayenne, salt and pepper. Spray the potatoes lightly with the olive oil spray and dust with the seasoning.

Rotate in the Flat Standard Basket for 30 to 40 minutes or until tender.

NUTRITIONAL ANALYSIS PER SERVING: 61 Calories, 12.4 g Carbohydrates, 1.4 g Protein, 0.75 g Fat, 0 mg Cholesterol, 4 mg Sodium

ROASTED POTATOES WITH FENNEL AND RED PEPPER

SERVES 4

2 medium fennel bulbs
2 cups cubed red potatoes
1 cup red bell pepper strips
1 small red onion, cut into 8 wedges
1 tablespoon olive oil
1/2 teaspoon dried basil
1/2 teaspoon dried marjoram
1/4 teaspoon salt
1/8 teaspoon freshly ground pepper
2 (14 x 12 inch) sheets heavy-duty aluminum foil

Trim tough outer leaves from fennel; remove and discard stalks. Cut fennel bulb into quarters lengthwise; discard core. Cut bulb into 1-inch pieces to measure 4 cups.

Combine fennel, potatoes, red pepper, red onion, olive oil, basil, marjoram, salt and pepper in a medium-size bowl; toss to coat vegetables with oil, herbs and spices. Turn vegetables out onto one sheet of foil. Top with second sheet of foil and fold edges over three times to seal the foil packet.

Rotate in the Flat Standard Basket for 40 minutes. Open packet and serve.

NUTRITIONAL ANALYSIS PER SERVING: 132 Calories, 21.9 g Carbohydrates, 4.5 g Protein, 3.9 g Fat, 9 mg Cholesterol, 161 mg Sodium

The LEAN Rotisserie

ROASTED ROOT VEGETABLES

SERVES 4

2 cups diagonally sliced parsnip
2 cups diagonally sliced carrots
1 3/4-pound rutabaga, peeled and cut into 1-inch pieces
2 tablespoons fresh lemon juice
2 teaspoons dried thyme
2 teaspoons olive oil
1/2 teaspoon salt
1/2 teaspoon pepper
2 (14 x 12 inch) sheets heavy-duty aluminum foil

In a medium-size bowl toss together all ingredients. Transfer vegetable mixture to one sheet of the foil. Top with second sheet of foil and fold edges over three times to seal the foil packet.

Rotate in the Flat Standard Basket for 50 minutes. Open packet and serve.

NUTRITIONAL ANALYSIS PER SERVING: 141 Calories, 28.9 g Carbohydrates, 2.7 g Protein, 2.8 g Fat, 0 mg Cholesterol, 337 mg Sodium

PASTA WITH
ROASTED VEGETABLES
SERVES 4 TO 6

1 zucchini, sliced in half lengthwise
1 small eggplant, peeled and cut in half lengthwise
1 small red onion, peeled and cut in half crosswise
1 red bell pepper, cut in half lengthwise, seeds removed
1/4 cup non-fat Italian salad dressing
2 tablespoons minced fresh basil
1/2 pound corkscrew-shaped pasta, cooked and drained

Prepare the vegetables. Brush vegetables with a light coating of the salad dressing. Rotate the vegetables in the Flat Standard Basket 20 minutes or until very tender.

Remove vegetables and coarsely chop. Toss with remaining salad dressing and basil. Place hot cooked pasta in a serving bowl and toss with vegetable mixture. Serve immediately, or cool and chill to serve as a salad.

NUTRITIONAL ANALYSIS PER SERVING: 248 Calories, 51 g Carbohydrates, 8.7 g Protein, 1.1 g Fat, 0 mg Cholesterol, 8 mg Sodium

HONEYED MANGOS WITH RUM

SERVES 6

3 tablespoons dark Rum
2 tablespoons honey
1/2 teaspoon minced lime zest
1 tablespoon fresh lime juice
1/8 teaspoon ground cinnamon
5 cups sliced peeled ripe mango (about 3 pounds)
2 (14 x 12 inch) sheets heavy-duty aluminum foil

Stir the Rum, honey, lime zest and juice with cinnamon in a small bowl. Arrange mango slices on one sheet of foil. Drizzle with Rum mixture. Top with second sheet of foil and fold edges over three times to seal the foil packet.

Rotate in the Flat Standard Basket for 20 minutes. Open packet and serve mango with juices.

NUTRITIONAL ANALYSIS PER SERVING: 112 Calories, 29.5 g Carbohydrates, 0.7 g Protein, 0.4 g Fat, 9 mg Cholesterol, 3 mg Sodium

ROASTED SUMMER FRUIT SALAD
SERVES 6

1-1/2 cups sliced peeled papaya
1-1/2 cups sliced peeled peaches or nectarines
3/4 cup cubed peeled ripe mango
1 tablespoon fresh lime juice
1 tablespoon butter, melted
1 teaspoon sugar
6 tablespoons balsamic vinegar
2 (14 x 12 inch) sheets heavy-duty aluminum foil

Lay papaya, peaches, and mango on one sheet of foil. Combine lime juice and melted butter and drizzle over fruit. Sprinkle with sugar. Top with second sheet of foil and fold edges over three times to seal the foil packet.

Rotate in the Flat Standard Basket for 20 minutes. Bring vinegar to a boil in a small saucepan and cook 3 minutes or until reduced to 1-1/2 tablespoons. Open fruit packet and serve fruit drizzled with balsamic vinegar reduction.

NUTRITIONAL ANALYSIS PER SERVING: 66 Calories, 12.8 g Carbohydrates, 0.6 g Protein, 2 g Fat, 10 mg Cholesterol, 24 mg Sodium

PINEAPPLE WITH
BASIL AND GINGER
SERVES 4 TO 6

1/4 cup honey
2 tablespoons cider vinegar
1 tablespoon finely chopped crystallized ginger
1 teaspoon dry basil
1 medium pineapple (about 3 pounds), peeled and cored
2 (14 x 12 inch) sheets heavy-duty aluminum foil

Stir together the honey, vinegar, ginger and basil in a small bowl. Cut the pineapple into 1/2-inch thick slices. Lay the pineapple slices overlapping on one sheet of foil. Drizzle with honey mixture. Top with second sheet of foil and fold edges over three times to seal the foil packet.

Rotate in the Flat Standard Basket for 20 minutes. Open packet and serve fruit with any juices.

NUTRITIONAL ANALYSIS PER SERVING: 133 Calories, 35 g Carbohydrates, 1 g Protein, 1 g Fat, 0 mg Cholesterol, 4 mg Sodium

APRICOT BAKED APPLES
SERVES 4

2 large apples
3 tablespoons fresh lemon juice
2 tablespoons apricot spreadable fruit
2 tablespoons chopped dried apricots
1 tablespoon finely chopped walnuts
2 (14 x 12 inch) sheets heavy-duty aluminum foil

Cut each apple in half lengthwise and remove the core. You may peel the apple or not. Lay the apples, cut side up, on one sheet of foil. Drizzle with lemon juice. Divide the jam evenly between the apples, spreading it on the cut surface. Sprinkle with dried apricots and walnuts. Top with second sheet of foil and fold edges over three times to seal the foil packet.

Rotate in the Flat Standard Basket for 30 minutes or until apples are tender. Open packet and serve apples with any juices.

NUTRITIONAL ANALYSIS PER SERVING: 109 Calories, 26.6 g Carbohydrates, 0.7 g Protein, 1.2 g Fat, 0 mg Cholesterol, 5 mg Sodium

The LEAN
Rotisserie

BRANDIED APRICOT HALVES
SERVES 4

1 (16 ounce) can unsweetened apricot halves, undrained
1/4 cup Brandy
Pinch cinnamon
2 (14 x 12 inch) sheets heavy-duty aluminum foil

Drain apricots, reserving 1/2 cup juice. Combine juice, Brandy and cinnamon in a small bowl. Lay apricot halves on one sheet of foil and drizzle with Brandy syrup. Top with second sheet of foil and fold edges over three times to seal the foil packet.

Rotate in the Flat Standard Basket for 15 minutes or until heated through. Open packet and serve apricot with juices.

NUTRITIONAL ANALYSIS PER SERVING: 86 Calories, 14 g Carbohydrates, 0.7 g Protein, 0.1 g Fat, 0 mg Cholesterol, 5 mg Sodium

PEACHES WITH CHEESE AND PISTACHIOS

SERVES 4

4 medium peaches, peeled and halved crosswise
1/2 cup part-skim ricotta cheese
2 tablespoons powdered sugar
1/8 teaspoon vanilla
4 teaspoons chopped toasted pistachio nuts

Rotate peaches in the Flat Standard Basket for 15 minutes or until tender and heated through. In a small bowl, combine the cheese, powdered sugar and vanilla. Spoon 1 tablespoon of the cheese mixture into the center of each peach half. Sprinkle with pistachio nuts and serve warm or cold.

NUTRITIONAL ANALYSIS PER SERVING: 138 Calories, 23.2 g Carbohydrates, 5.1 g Protein, 3.7 g Fat, 10 mg Cholesterol, 39 mg Sodium

The LEAN
Rotisserie

SPICED PLUMS
SERVES 4

4 plums, halved
1/2 cup fresh orange juice
1/4 cup brown sugar
1/2 teaspoon ground cinnamon
1/8 teaspoon freshly grated nutmeg
1/8 teaspoon ground cumin
1/8 teaspoon ground cardamom
1 tablespoon slivered toasted almonds
2 (14 x 12 inch) sheets heavy-duty aluminum foil

Place plums on one sheet of the foil. Stir together the orange juice, brown sugar and spices. Pour over plums. Top with second sheet of foil and fold edges over three times to seal the foil packet.

Rotate in the Flat Standard Basket for 20 minutes. Open packet and serve with juices, sprinkled with toasted nuts.

NUTRITIONAL ANALYSIS PER SERVING: 96 Calories, 21.4 g Carbohydrates, 1.1 g Protein, 1.4 g Fat, 9 mg Cholesterol, 4 mg Sodium

LIGHT & LUSCIOUS MAPLE PEARS
SERVES 4

4 large Anjou or Bosc pears
1/4 cup real maple syrup
1 tablespoon toasted sliced almonds
2 (14 x 12 inch) sheets heavy-duty aluminum foil

Peel the pears, cut in half lengthwise and core. Lay pears on one sheet of foil and drizzle with maple syrup. Top with second sheet of foil and fold edges over three times to seal the foil packet. Rotate in the Flat Standard Basket for 30 minutes or until pears are tender. Open packet and serve sprinkled with toasted nuts.

NUTRITIONAL ANALYSIS PER SERVING: 181 Calories, 45 g Carbohydrates, 1 g Protein, 1.3 g Fat, 0 mg Cholesterol, 2 mg Sodium

RASPBERRY PINEAPPLE WEDGES
SERVES 4

1 fresh pineapple
4 tablespoons raspberry syrup
4 sprigs fresh mint

Peel the pineapple and cut into 8 wedges, lengthwise. Cut off the core. Rotate the pineapple in the Flat Standard Basket for about 10 minutes or until warmed through and lightly browned. Transfer to serving plates and drizzle with syrup. Garnish with mint.

NUTRITIONAL ANALYSIS PER SERVING: 83 Calories, 21 g Carbohydrates, 0.3 g Protein, 0.3 g Fat, 0 mg Cholesterol, 3 mg Sodium

BANANAS WITH BROWN SUGAR-WALNUT GLAZE

SERVES 6

1/3 cup brown sugar
1/4 cup fresh lemon juice
2 tablespoons reduced-calorie margarine, melted
1/4 teaspoon ground cinnamon
4 large firm ripe bananas
1/4 cup chopped walnuts, toasted
1-1/2 cups vanilla lowfat frozen yogurt
2 (14 x 12 inch) sheets heavy-duty aluminum foil

Combine the brown sugar, lemon juice, melted margarine and cinnamon in a small bowl. Cut bananas in half lengthwise. Place banana halves, cut sides up, on one sheet of foil. Drizzle with sugar mixture and walnuts. Top with second sheet of foil and fold edges over three times to seal the foil packet.

Rotate in the Flat Standard Basket for 20 minutes. Open packet and serve fruit with any juices and topped with frozen yogurt.

NUTRITIONAL ANALYSIS PER SERVING: 237 Calories, 44.5 g Carbohydrates, 3.9 g Protein, 7 g Fat, 5 mg Cholesterol, 58 mg Sodium

HOT PAPAYA SUNDAES

SERVES 4

2 small firm ripe papayas (about 1 pound each)
1 tablespoon butter, melted
1/2 teaspoon minced lime zest
1/3 cup Rum or water
1/4 cup lime juice
3 tablespoons honey
2 cups lowfat vanilla frozen yogurt

Cut papayas in half, peel and seed them. Brush papayas with melted butter and rotate in the Flat Standard Basket for 15 minutes or until warmed through.

Meanwhile, heat the lime zest, Rum, lime juice and honey in a small saucepan until boiling. Transfer papayas to serving dishes and pour syrup over all. Top each papaya with a scoop of frozen yogurt and serve immediately.

NUTRITIONAL ANALYSIS PER SERVING: 279 Calories, 47 g Carbohydrates, 5 g Protein, 4 g Fat, 5 mg Cholesterol, 96 mg Sodium